Instructo[illegible]

MW01711683

International Herald Tribune
Published With The New York Times and The Washington Post

IN THE NEWS

Ethel Tiersky
Maxine Chernoff

National Textbook Company
NTC a division of *NTC Publishing Group* • Lincolnwood, Illinois USA

Articles from the *International Herald Tribune* are republished by permission of the International Herald Tribune, 181 avenue Charles-de-Gaulle, 92200 Neuilly-sur-Seine, France; The New York Times; and The Washington Post, the copyright proprietors.

1994 Printing

Published by National Textbook Company, a division of NTC Publishing Group, 4255 West Touhy Avenue, Lincolnwood (Chicago), Illinois 60646-1975 U.S.A.

Manufactured in the United States of America.

3 4 5 6 7 8 9 0 VP 9 8 7 6 5 4 3 2

CONTENTS

Introduction

OVERVIEW

In the News: Mastering Reading and Language Skills with the Newspaper is a reading text designed to help students improve their reading mastery and their language skills. Based on the premise that a newspaper is an excellent tool for teaching reading strategies and improving language fluency, the text offers thirty challenging, high-interest articles taken directly from the pages of the *International Herald Tribune*. The articles are organized into seven general areas, which correspond to standard newspaper sections: (1) News, (2) Opinion, (3) Business, (4) Education, (5) Arts and Leisure, (6) Science and Environment and (7) Sports. The text can be used by students of English as a Second Language (ESL) or by students of English as a Foreign Language (EFL), as well as by native English speakers.

The articles are accompanied by a variety of supporting exercises. A major goal of the exercises is to facilitate students' understanding of the articles: for example, comprehension exercises focus on helping students determine an article's main points, and the vocabulary and idiom exercises give students assistance in understanding key words and idioms. The exercises also provide opportunities for students to talk and write about issues raised by the articles. Thus, the text uses an approach that integrates reading, critical analysis, discussion and writing, letting students employ a wide array of language skills.

Finally, special sections, called *Focus on the Newspaper*, are designed to familiarize students with the content and organization of newspapers and help students develop personal strategies for reading the newspaper.

Becoming a habitual reader of the *International Herald Tribune* or another daily newspaper is one of the best ways for students to develop their reading and English language skills. This text offers an important message: Become an active newspaper reader. And it gives students the tools and strategies needed to do so.

About the Student Text

Varied, High-Interest Articles: The thirty articles in the text, which cover a wide variety of topics, provide students with the opportunity to use their previous understanding of subjects in the news while expanding their knowledge of cultural trends, technological innovations, and current events. Do students, for instance, know that a new leisure activity based on sky diving has developed in crowded Tokyo? Do they realize that the 500th anniversary of Christopher Columbus's arrival in North America has been greeted with mixed reviews by the culturally diverse U.S. population? Have they ever been curious about the motivation of downhill skiers to challenge mountains in that dangerous sport?

Since *In the News* is a general text, care has been taken to select articles that will engage most students. The articles are designed to pique students' interest and possibly even to broaden it.

Further designed to draw students' attention and interest are the visuals accompanying the articles. The photos and cartoons often serve to illustrate key points of the article. One article employs a graph to supplement the text. All the visual material provides another source for discussion. In fact, among educators, the concept of "visual literacy" has now been added to the possible ways that a person can comprehend material.

Authentic Material: The readings in this text have not been simplified for the students. Rather, students work with the original language of the newspaper article with its natural, idiomatic use of English vocabulary. Students' mastery is ensured by the extensive materials that accompany the article, define key words and idioms, and allow students to check and fine-tune their comprehension. Having successfully read the articles should give students the confidence they need to read English-language newspapers on their own.

Multicultural Information: Because of the variety of cultures and settings in the articles—from the art of the Inuit Eskimo to a trip to a Japanese barbershop—students will have opportunities to expand their knowledge of other cultures, as well as to discuss multicultural issues. The broad-ranging readings should lead to lively discussions of cultural differences and similarities, as well as of cultural change.

The Exercises: As previously mentioned, a variety of exercises accompanies the article, many of which will help students better comprehend the article and the key points the author is making. Here are some of the exercise types:

- Prereading exercises

  These provide helpful background to stimulate students' interest, invite students to discuss what they already know about the topic, and establish reading objectives.

- Comprehension exercises

  Each article has a short objective exercise that allows students to immediately measure how well they understood the article, checking their answers on their own. In addition, there often are more open-ended comprehension exercises that require critical thinking, for example, calling on students to summarize main points or classify information into charts.

- Vocabulary exercises

  Each article has an exercise that asks students to define key words using context clues, thus building students' vocabulary acquisition strategies. Most articles also have exercises that define key idioms and ask students to use them in context. There may be additional vocabulary exercises; for example, ones that have students practice useful vocabulary or analyze word parts.

- Analysis exercises

  These help students analyze grammar and sentence structure (e.g., adjective clauses, pronouns, contrast words), main ideas in paragraphs or author's tone and style.

- Discussion and writing exercises

  These encourage students to give their reactions to the articles and to the issues raised in the articles. They can be used as the basis for both class discussion and individual writing assignments.

For concrete suggestions for using the exercises in the classroom and a more detailed explanation of their rationale, see "Techniques for Implementing the Text" in this Introduction.

Focus on the Newspaper Sections: The eight *Focus on the Newspaper* sections are invitations to students to pick up a daily paper and begin applying their skills. These hands-on sessions encourage students to keep logs on newspaper reading, classify article types, look for main ideas, make predictions from photos and headlines and even analyze ads. Some students may already be performing these activities less formally in their everyday reading. For others, the experience will be new. For suggestions on using the *Focus on the Newspaper* sections in the classroom, see "Techniques for Implementing the Text" on page 5 in this Introduction.

About the Instructor's Manual

In addition to the student text, there is this detailed *Instructor's Manual*, consisting of three sections.

The Introduction: The first section, the Introduction, familiarizes you with the student text and with the *Instructor's Manual.* Handy tips on implementing the text and on teaching reading skills in general are provided. The Introduction also outlines how best for your students to use and how *not* to use a dictionary.

Guidelines for Teaching the Articles: The second section provides you with article-by-article teaching tips. These typically include:

- extensive background notes on the articles, including definitions of key terms when pertinent
- a list of related readings in the text and outside the text for students to explore
- suggested audiovisual aids for teachers to provide to accompany the article

In addition, the article-by-article discussion also contains suggestions to help students develop language and reading ability, supplementing the exercises in the student text. The following sections are typically included:

- reading skills
- word study
- numbers and measurements
- style and tone

Finally, there is a variety of extended activities that recommend group projects, further research, visual and listening experiences, as well as field trips and demonstrations that can enhance students' involvement with the text.

How many or how few of these activities you choose to present, of course, will depend both on your schedule and on the context in which you are using *In the News.*

Exercise Answers: The third section of the *Instructor's Manual* provides answers to the exercises in the student text. These can save you time in preparing to teach the text and can provide independent students with invaluable, direct feedback.

About the Audiocassettes

Also available is a set of three audiocassettes with selected articles from the text recorded on them. Included on the cassettes are the articles in the News section and at least two articles from each of the other sections.

The cassettes can be used in a variety of ways:

- As presentation material: You might play parts of the articles as part of previewing the article to introduce students to the topic.
- For self-study: Students might want to listen to the articles independently after reading them to improve comprehension and pronunciation skills.
- As listening comprehension material: Play parts of the cassettes and have students listen for specific information; for example, information involving statistics.

TECHNIQUES FOR IMPLEMENTING THE TEXT

Because what students learn in class can be just as significant as what they gain from the text, *In the News* can be used as the basis for a high level of classroom interaction: readers share their knowledge of the topic of the article with other students and express their opinions and reactions.

Newspaper articles have two important advantages in a reading class. First, they are rather short and can be discussed in detail in one class period. Second, they are timely and therefore often of widespread interest.

Students should be encouraged to think about why each of these articles appeared in the newspaper at the particular time it did. Sometimes the information is stated in the article (there was a scientific conference and so on); sometimes the reason is easily inferred (near New Year's Day an article about New Year's customs is timely). Students should try to tie the reading to some happening that made it newsworthy at that time.

Presenting the Articles

The following part contains an outline for presenting the articles in class and implementing the accompanying exercises. The exercises for each article in the text follow a definite pattern. The rationale for each type of exercise and suggestions for implementing them effectively in class are discussed here.

Previewing the Article

The *Previewing the Article* section is designed to accomplish three main purposes: (1) stimulate interest in the reading, (2) provide explanations that help students understand the reading, and (3) encourage students to discuss the topic and share their knowledge about it. *Previewing the Article* contains topics for classroom discussion prior to the reading, and it helps the student to realize that the information in the article may have some relevance to his or her own life, past, present or future. Teachers should refer to the illustration accompanying the article (where there is one) and the article headline in the discussion.

Each *Previewing the Article* concludes with one or two suggestions regarding specific information that students should look for while reading the newspaper article. You should return to these concluding questions after the students' first reading to see if they have found the information.

As part of the preview, it is helpful to bring a map of the specific places discussed in the article. Students should know where the article takes place as they begin to read. In addition, you might want to present some of the background information for the article given in "Specific Suggestions for Teaching the Articles" in this Instructor's Manual.

Introducing the Newspaper Article: In conjunction with doing the *Previewing the Article* activities, here are some general suggestions for introducing the actual text of the article for student reading.

In general, the most difficult parts of each article are the headline and the first paragraph. In many of these, the journalist, in order to attract readers' attention, has played with the language and perhaps used a pun or a variation of a well-known saying. Some students (especially nonnative speakers of English) may not "get" the reference or the double meaning. Therefore, we recommend that you read the headline and the first and second paragraphs aloud and have students restate in their own words what they have read.

Then students should make predictions about the content of the article: What questions will the article raise or answer? What will its main point be?

The next step can be to have students read the rest of the article and summarize its contents. At this point, some teachers may want to ask students specific questions, while others may choose to wait until after students have had a chance to reread and analyze the material themselves.

Reading a difficult article can be viewed as a game, a kind of decoding of a message. Teachers can take the fun and the surprise out of reading if they reveal too much too soon. Students should not be deprived of the challenge and the sense of accomplishment that can come from decoding the text independently. Therefore, after getting them started, you may want to send them home to tackle the rest of the piece on their own.

Note that the paragraphs in the text have been numbered for easy reference during classroom discussion and for completion of the exercises. Point out to students that, when writing newspaper material that will be printed in a narrow column, journalists tend to keep their paragraphs short. Material that might be one paragraph in a magazine or book may be written as two or three paragraphs in a newspaper column. Therefore, when reading a newspaper, students should not consider the end of a paragraph as a signal of a major shift in thought.

Emphasize whether the article about to be read is supposed to be objective coverage of a news event or the writer's opinion. Students should realize that, within an objective news story, there may be opinions that the journalist is quoting, but these are not the author's opinions. Objective journalism should quote or paraphrase opinions on both sides of an issue, giving fairly equal space to each in order to provide balanced coverage. Students can evaluate news stories to see if they are really objective. On the other hand, editorials and reviews are supposed to be opinion. However, the opinion should be supported by specific reasons or evidence.

Getting the Message

Getting the Message contains one or two exercises. The answers to the first exercise, which is always an objective exercise, are in the back of the student text. These answers provide a chance for students to find out right away if they are correctly interpreting the text. Point out the location of these answers in the text. Encourage students to complete the exercise before looking at the answers. When students get an answer wrong, they should go back to the newspaper article, reread the relevant paragraph(s), and make sure that they find out why their original answer was wrong.

In *Getting the Message*, the exercise styles vary. The first exercise is usually multiple choice or true-false. The second usually is a more open-ended one that often requires critical thinking and that may require writing sentences. A variety of reading skills are involved in doing these exercises, including scanning for specific information and noting reasons, examples and results. In several chapters, one of the exercises in this section is for students to complete a chart to classify information from the article or to check off the correct answers. In some exercises, students are asked to summarize major points in their own words.

Expanding Your Vocabulary

The first exercise in the Vocabulary part is always *Getting Meaning from Context.* This is a good exercise to assign for homework since students need independent practice in this skill. Remind students that the idea is to get the meaning from context, not the dictionary. After each word or phrase listed, there is a number (or perhaps two numbers) referring them to the paragraph in which the word or phrase was used. Students should go back to that paragraph for clues to the answer.

To help students develop the skill of determining meaning from context, it might be a good idea to do one or two of the items in class for the first few articles they read. Students can then share information about what part of the paragraph gave them the answer. When working at home, students who get "stuck" can use the dictionary as a last resort, but then, once they know the answer, they should go back to the paragraph to see where they could have found the answer in the text.

Expanding Your Vocabulary sometimes contains an exercise entitled *Reading for Suggested Meanings.* The questions encourage students to look beyond what is directly stated and make inferences about the meanings of various words, phrases and clauses. These questions are quite difficult, especially for nonnative speakers of English. In ESL/EFL classes, this inference exercise is best done in class, perhaps in pairs or small groups.

Other exercises in this section vary from article to article. Some of them deal with the meanings of phrases and even clauses, encouraging students to read groups of words rather than word by word. Some exercises provide practice with antonyms and synonyms. Some require students to think about word categories and circle words that don't fit into a stated category. Some require students to analyze word parts.

You can use the vocabulary exercises in a variety of ways. Students can work on them individually at home or in pairs during class. The group can then go over the answers, and questions can be answered.

It is a good idea to pronounce the words with students, especially nonnative speakers. Students can also be encouraged to figure out correct pronunciation by reading dictionary symbols.

After students have studied the words in *Expanding Your Vocabulary*, make a game out of the words. This can be something as simple as matching synonyms or filling in blanks in sentences. Have students work in teams to see who wins.

Working with Idioms

All or most of the idioms found in the article are defined in *Working with Idioms*. (This activity may not appear if an article has few idioms that might cause students problems.) The definitions given are the ones used in the particular article. If an idiom listed has other common meanings, you may wish to point them out to students. After each idiom, there is a number in parentheses, which gives the paragraph reference. This section is particularly valuable (and difficult) for nonnative speakers of English. However, teachers may be surprised to discover that it also teaches something new to native speakers.

American English idioms may be unfamiliar to native speakers of British English, and British idioms may be unfamiliar to Americans. Also, some idioms may be regional, substandard or literary and therefore not familiar to all of your students.

In some idiom sections, phrasal verbs are listed separately. The presentation is primarily concerned with teaching the meaning of the verbs. However, in classes for nonnative speakers, teachers may want to go into matters of sentence structure and word order, illustrating and having students practice separable and inseparable phrasal verbs.

In ESL/EFL classes, it is a good idea to introduce the idioms before the students tackle the reading.

Making Sense of Sentences, Analyzing Paragraphs and Focusing on Style and Tone

The next activity part in each chapter is one of the following: *Making Sense of Sentences*, *Analyzing Paragraphs* or *Focusing on Style and Tone*. These activities encourage students to analyze the text more deeply.

Making Sense of Sentences deals with a wide variety of sentence structures. The main goal is to be sure that students understand the meaning of the structure. To help students master the various sentence patterns, some of these exercises ask students to write (or complete) sentences in a pattern used in the newspaper article. Some of the sentence structures practiced in these sections are the following: literal comparisons with *-er*, *more*, and *less*; *if* statements, both future possible and contrary to fact; relative clauses with *who* (restrictive and nonrestrictive) and *whose*; complex and compound sentences that express contrast with *but, still, although* and *while*; *because* clauses before and after the main clause; pronoun reference; and sentences using *not only . . . but also*. Since you want every student to get this writing practice, these exercises should be assigned as homework, or (with less capable classes) done individually in class, with your assistance.

Analyzing Paragraphs helps students analyze the main points or key points of paragraphs, and become familiar with various types of paragraph development (comparison and contrast; cause and effect; examples; and so on). Questions are designed to improve reading comprehension by calling attention to what particular paragraphs contribute to the whole, what information they give and how. Some articles present two sides of an issue. Students are asked to note which paragraphs present information to support each side. For example, in one exercise, students are introduced to the rebuttal paragraph, in which the author presents the opposing side's view and then points out its weaknesses.

Focusing on Style and Tone deals with the uses of irony, figurative language and negative and positive word connotations. Here, as in other sections, students are helped to notice implied ideas. Techniques of overall organization are also noted, as are various ways of developing an article based upon a journalistic interview.

Talking and Writing

Talking and Writing, the last exercise section, accompanies every article. It offers two to four topics for class discussion. One of these can become the topic of a writing assignment, either a paragraph or an essay, at the teacher's discretion. Many of these topics encourage students to relate the newspaper article to their personal experiences or respond to the article with an opinion or comparison. In some chapters, one of the choices for writing involves some library research to find out more about some aspect or extension of the topic. The suggested writings provide students with opportunities to practice many different types of paragraphs and compositions. Some topics lead to narrative pieces based upon personal experiences. Others involve comparison and contrast, cause and effect or the use of examples.

For reading and word study exercises to supplement those in the text, as well as suggested extension activities, refer to "Guidelines for Teaching the Articles" section in this Instructor's Manual.

Presenting the *Focus on the Newspaper* Sections

Becoming a habitual reader of the *International Herald Tribune* or another daily newspaper is one of the best ways for nonnative speakers to become more fluent and competent in English. For those students whose native language is English, the *Focus on the Newspaper* sections provide a nonthreatening way to make the transition from reading the text to reading a major daily newspaper. There are eight *Focus on the Newspaper* sections. The first serves as an introduction to newspaper reading and the others follow each of the seven sections of the text, relating to the subject of the section. They stress approaches that will make your students comfortable reading the newspaper in English as a daily activity after their work in the student text is completed.

All of the activities must be completed with a newspaper in hand. They sometimes involve materials that are associated with younger learners: scissors, marking pens and tape or glue, for clipping and collecting articles and logging and highlighting main ideas.

Although the seven specific newspaper applications are placed at the end of each appropriate section, they might also serve to introduce a section. Therefore, you may want to use the *Focus on the Newspaper* activities to begin each section of the text. However, since the newspaper exercises sometimes build on or reinforce skills learned in the articles themselves, you may feel it more appropriate to use them at the close of a section.

Many of the *Focus on the Newspaper* exercises can be completed outside of class. The exercises provide a natural way to move newspaper activities beyond the classroom and into the students' home setting, where newspapers are most often and naturally read. At home, the student can most easily collect certain articles, search for selected themes, and compose mock letters to the editor. Of course, follow-up work and discussion about the activities should be done in class.

However, most of the activities lend themselves to group work and discussion in class as well. Small-group work can be initiated around some of the activities. For example, students can share analysis of political cartoons in the *Focus on the Newspaper: Opinion* section. They can track and sell stocks in the *Focus on the Newspaper: Business* section. These activities invite group collaboration and shared comparisons.

Whichever method or combination of methods you choose, students should be made to feel that each *Focus on the Newspaper* section is an interesting, hands-on experience. These sections provide an excellent tool to help your students make a transition from reading material that has been carefully selected for them within the text to choosing appropriate newspaper reading material for themselves.

The first *Focus on the Newspaper* (pages 1 to 4 in the text) presents an overview of the organization and contents of daily newspapers. It invites students to work singly or in pairs to locate useful information in the newspaper such as weather and advertisements, to become acquainted with newspaper terms such as *dateline* and *headline* and to analyze their own newspaper reading habits. This self-analysis leads them to begin a newspaper reading log, an activity that is repeated in different forms in the later *Focus* sections.

Focus on the Newspaper: News (pages 23 and 24 in the text) presents the typical journalistic questions, *who*, *what*, *where*, *when*, *why* and *how*, in a news context. It illustrates the "reverse pyramid" construction of the news article, in which most of the pertinent information is offered in the first few sentences or paragraphs, since newspaper articles often have to be cut for space reasons. The section asks students to complete a skimming exercise to help analyze the structure of news articles. Then students make their own choice of a news article to analyze in more detail. Finally, students use critical thinking to extend the content of the article. As "editors," they provide a follow-up assignment for another article based on guidelines presented in the exercise.

Focus on the Newspaper: Opinion (pages 48 to 50 in the text) introduces the contrast between objective and subjective content in the newspaper. It asks students to consider points of view and directs them to notice the types of material that editorial pages often contain. Students formulate the main idea of an editorial they have selected and express their own opinion on the topic. In addition, editorial cartoons and letters to the editor are analyzed in varied activities.

Focus on the Newspaper: Business (pages 73 and 74 in the text) introduces various topics discussed in business sections and has students analyze a business article. It asks students to locate essential vocabulary for the reader of the business section. Students analyze economic trends and chart the progress of a stock of their choice on the market over a two-week period.

Focus on the Newspaper: Education (pages 95 and 96 in the text) asks readers to consider aspects of early childhood, school and adult education. It introduces issues commonly treated in education articles and asks students to analyze an education article. They look at problems in education, predict their solutions and analyze their attitudes about the problems. In addition, this section contains advertisements for educational programs, which students analyze and use as the basis for a writing exercise.

Focus on the Newspaper: Arts and Leisure (pages 121 and 122 in the text) examines the reviews of cultural events and profiles of famous people in the art and entertainment world. With references to high and low culture—from art exhibits to rock stars—it asks readers to log and examine two typical article types in arts and leisure sections: the review and the profile.

Focus on the Newspaper: Science and Environment (pages 144 and 145 in the text) discusses how journalists make technical material relevant to the average reader. It asks students to analyze a scientific article by type of development. It also has students evaluate an ecological article for content, focus and objectivity. Issues of point of view and bias are discussed in the context of ecology articles. Finally, it has students analyze an article that treats health.

Focus on the Newspaper: Sports (pages 167 and 168 in the text) examines the news, profiles, business deals and scores that are contained within a typical sports section. It asks the students to analyze sports articles, including articles relating to a sports event that just took place or that is about to take place, as well as profiles of sports figures. It also examines the colorful language of sports stories.

All of these *Focus* sections provide the reader with valuable newspaper experience. For sophisticated readers comfortable with the newspaper, they refine newspaper reading skills in English. For uninitiated newspaper readers, they introduce the elements of critical newspaper reading in an active, supportive manner.

GENERAL SUGGESTIONS FOR THE READING TEACHER

What are the essential elements of the reading experience? There is an author who writes something for an audience of readers. These three ingredients—author, written work, and reader—must all be considered by the reading teacher as new material is presented to students. Students must be encouraged to consider (1) the nature of the work itself, (2) the author's relationship to the work and (3) their own interaction with the topic and content. This last element can be further divided into two parts: (a) what background the student brings to the reading and (b) what the student takes from the work (new information, a change in attitude and so on).

The Author's Authority: Unfortunately, all too many readers assume that whatever appears in print is true. Students should be encouraged to be skeptical readers. "Who wrote this, and what's his or her background?" That's a key question students should ask. The discriminating reader wants some reassurance that the author knows what he or she is talking about. Is the author an expert in the field, or has he or she consulted experts to get information? Is the author writing from direct experience or first-hand observation? How much does the author know about the subject? These are fair questions, and they lead to general questions like the following: Do you think the author's facts and/or implications are correct? Do you agree with his or her opinions? Are the author's conclusions reasonable, based upon the information given?

The Author's Bias: Perceptive readers learn to consider what an author says in terms of that person's relationship to the subject matter. A magazine article written about the importance of banning the sale of handguns is quite different if the author is the owner of a gun shop, a law enforcement officer, or the mother of a young man recently killed in a drive-by shooting. Is the material striving to be objective or is it admittedly and openly subjective? Of course, it is difficult to write something that is completely objective. Often the author's attitude sneaks into the piece in subtle ways. For example, if the article presents two sides of some public debate, which one does the author give more space to? Do word connotations reveal a negative attitude toward one side or the other? Looking for the author's bias can be fun and enlightening.

The Reader's Background: In recent years, educators have become increasingly aware of the fact that the reader is not simply a passive recipient of reading material. Every reader brings certain experiences, attitudes, interests and biases to the material. Some readers come to a reading with much greater understanding of the topic than others. As a result, what one reader might describe as boring another will find fascinating. Part of the reading teacher's job is to bridge a gap that might be a barrier to comprehension, appreciation and enjoyment. One of the functions of prereading activities is to allow the teacher and the students to share information and experiences, so that all students will bring enough background to the reading to understand it.

The Reader's Development: What does the student take away from the reading? Unfortunately, sometimes the answer is "very little." Part of the teacher's job is to help each student make the reading a part of his or her experiences in some way. Passive reading is often inadequately understood and quickly forgotten. How can the teacher make students into active, involved readers? It is, first of all, a good idea to assign readings that have some relevance to the lives of the student readers. But, beyond that, a teacher should encourage students to do something with the information read. Some possibilities are (1) retelling (summarizing) the material in their own words, (2) using material that presents two sides as the basis for a classroom debate, (3) doing further research on the topic, independently or with a small group, (4) working with a partner on comprehension exercises, or (5) critiquing the piece of writing.

It is unfortunate but true: students' preconceived attitudes influence what they learn and retain from a reading. As is true of many people in all kinds of situations, they see what they want to see. For example, the student text contains a reading about a law passed by the state of Iowa that banned smoking by minors. In an advanced ESL class that was classroom-testing this manuscript, most of the students concluded that the law was a good idea. Their logic? Smoking is bad for people; therefore, any law that forbids it must be good.

In reading the Iowa smoking article, most students ignored all the evidence, presented by experienced law enforcement professionals, that the law wouldn't work, that it was unenforceable. It is important to encourage students to consider ideas that contradict prior assumptions. There is almost no point in reading if a person does so only to seek reinforcement of beliefs already held.

How can teachers help students determine what to accept as well supported? Readers should search for evidence that supports the author's assertions. Supporting details such as statistics, examples, causes, reasons, definitions, comparisons and results are what to look for. The next job is to evaluate these. One example of a child who is unhappy because mother has a full-time job does not prove that all children of working mothers are lonely and unhappy. The author may assert that a particular effect resulted from a particular cause. The critical reader should then look for proof of the cause-effect relationship. The author's logic must be analyzed before it is accepted as valid.

THE ROLE OF THE DICTIONARY IN A READING CLASS

You will notice (and perhaps be surprised) that some exercises in the student text and suggested activities in the Instructor's Manual encourage the use of a dictionary. Many reading teachers discourage dictionary usage for some very good reasons. Every reading teacher is familiar with the diligent student who spends more time reading the dictionary than anything else. Each time a new word appears, the student puts down the reading material and runs to the dictionary. By the time the student has finished reading five paragraphs, tedious time has gone by, and the passage is so marked up with definitions that the original text is no longer readable. Moreover, the student is exhausted and confused. As the common expression goes, he or she has lost sight of the forest and seen only the trees. Obviously, the reading teacher wants to discourage this kind of slavish dependence on a dictionary. The student should be encouraged to read for main ideas, note relationships between ideas, make intelligent guesses of word meanings from context, and seek meaning from phrases and clauses rather than individual words. The text provides exercises to develop these kinds of reading skills.

How can teachers help students break the habit of using the dictionary as a crutch? Teach this motto: Keep reading! On the first reading of an article, students should *not* stop to look up new words. The meanings may become clear as the student progresses through the article. At any rate, the initial reading should be for grasping the main ideas and for determining the general purpose of the work. On the second reading, the student should underline unfamiliar words (particularly those that seem essential to understanding the article) and try to determine their meanings from context clues. In a reading class, students can share their ideas about what the difficult words mean, based upon their guesses from context. After that, it is interesting for students to check the dictionary and see how close the guesses were. Once students see that they can, in fact, determine meaning from context, they should feel less dependent upon the dictionary.

Nevertheless, used intelligently and in moderation, the dictionary is a wonderful tool for digging more meaning out of a written text. The English language has close to a million words, if one counts technical words specific to particular occupations. There is no such thing as complete mastery of the language. Students may be surprised to learn that even well-educated adult native speakers of English probably hear or read several words a week that are unfamiliar to them. Some people ignore them, getting meaning from context and doing just fine. Others, people who could be called word junkies, eagerly grab onto a new word and won't let it go until it has revealed its meaning, via a dictionary or a helpful friend. We hope that the exercises and activities suggested in this student text and Instructor's Manual will help to turn some of your students into word junkies. It is fascinating to investigate word origins and note the relationships between words that contain the same prefixes, roots or suffixes. Learning one word part can add many words to a student's vocabulary. Therefore, we encourage lexical research as broadening and entertaining. One of the pleasures of reading material from fine newspapers is to note how cleverly the journalists handle the language. To fully appreciate this, students do need to use a dictionary from time to time.

What dictionary? For these readings, a pocket-size dictionary will not be adequate. Students should use a desk-size college dictionary, which offers access to more information about each word and also a much greater number of words. Occasionally, they may even need to refer to an unabridged dictionary, if the author uses an obscure word (such as *whoosh* in the article about Karen Bennett's gallbladder surgery in the text).

To help students get the most from a standard desk dictionary, it is a good idea to ask all the students to purchase such a dictionary and then teach them how to use it. Encourage them to read the introduction, study the pronunciation symbols and note the organization. (For example, are people and places listed with common nouns or separately in the back of the dictionary?) Most students, even native speakers of English, do not realize how much information there is in a dictionary. Show students where to find syllable division, preferred spellings, levels of usage and irregular inflections of nouns, verbs and adjectives. Point out the key to the abbreviations, so that they can understand the information about word origins and parts of speech. Most important, be sure they know the logic behind the order of the definitions in the particular dictionary they are using. Does the dictionary begin with the most commonly used contemporary meaning, the most general meaning or the earliest meaning (which is what historical dictionaries do)?

Nonnative speakers of English should not expect to find all the definitions they need in a bilingual dictionary. Such dictionaries are quite limited. Dictionaries written specifically for ESL/EFL students are fine, as far as they go. But many words used in these articles are not common enough to be in ESL/EFL dictionaries. Nonnative speakers should also consult a standard English dictionary. Since most of these articles were written by Americans for an American newspaper, a dictionary of American English (rather than

British English) is likely to prove most helpful. A good dictionary of idioms and phrasal verbs is also a useful tool for nonnative speakers to have.

This text contains a wide range of subject matter, which means that students will be exposed to vocabulary and idioms from many different fields. A close reading of these articles and the sophisticated language they employ will help students to read the newspaper with less effort and greater understanding in the future.

Guidelines for Teaching the Articles

SECTION 1: NEWS

News: Article 1

Smokers Under 18 in Iowa Now Outlaws

BACKGROUND

A 150,000-word report issued by the Surgeon General of the United States in 1964 stated that "cigarette smoking is a health hazard of sufficient importance in the United States to warrant appropriate remedial action." Since then, the medical community, educators and health awareness groups have been trying to lower the rate of smoking-related deaths, which number 500,000 a year in the United States alone and 2 million worldwide. Packages of cigarettes sold in the U.S. now carry one of the following warning labels: "Smoking Causes Lung Cancer, Heart Disease, Emphysema, and May Complicate Pregnancy"; "Cigarette Smoke Contains Carbon Monoxide"; and "Quitting Smoking Now Greatly Reduces Serious Risks to Your Health."

Although some people have heeded these warnings and stopped smoking, new people take up the habit each day. A greater percentage of women have started to smoke in recent decades, and their death rate as the result of lung cancer has increased threefold. Teens have also taken up smoking, which many of them see as a sign of maturity and freedom from parental supervision. Many studies show a strong relationship between the age when smoking begins and the eventual chance of death from lung cancer. One study sponsored by the American Cancer Society revealed that men who had begun smoking between 15 and 19 years of age had twice the lung cancer mortality of those who began smoking between 20 and 24 and five times that of those who first smoked after age 25.

In the United States, many public service commercials, health classes in schools and laws such as the one discussed in this article try to discourage teens from beginning this destructive habit. Though many critics see antismoking laws as unenforceable, most people agree that health education is necessary to reduce the soaring death rate from tobacco consumption.

Nonsmokers in the United States have recently gotten involved as well in establishing local laws that ban smoking in public places and at work. It has been found that passive smoking (by being near a smoker) can also harm one's health.

Of course, the smoking habit is universal, as is the problem. Many countries are trying to reduce tobacco use among their citizens. As evidence of this, by 1985 more than 30,000 studies condemning smoking had been published worldwide. Yet smoking remains the single most preventable cause of illness and premature death in the United States and Europe.

Smoking tobacco is an old habit. American Indians smoked tobacco, primarily in pipes. With the discovery of the New World, the smoking habit spread to Europe in the 1500s. Pipe and cigar smoking were the more popular forms of tobacco use until this century when cigarette smoking became fashionable. Despite the warnings against smoking, it is estimated that 30 percent of all Americans smoke and that the statistics are even higher in some European countries.

RELATED READINGS

Articles in the Text: Another article that deals with unhealthy life-style trends is the article on meat consumption by Jeremy Rifkin, "Hold Your Nose at the Steak House," in the Opinion section. It might be discussed in connection with this article.

Items in the News: There are countless news stories about smoking and its effects. Recently in the United States, for instance, the widower of a woman who died of lung cancer sued a tobacco company for contributing to her death, a case briefly referred to in paragraph 16 of the article. Encourage students to clip other smoking stories and discuss the issues the articles raise.

AUDIOVISUAL AIDS

Many health education associations distribute antismoking posters or sponsor antismoking advertisements. Bring one to class and discuss it. You might also want to clip magazine ads that emphasize the glamour of smoking and discuss them with the class. Have students debate which posters or ads present their message most effectively.

- The article is recorded on the audiocassettes accompanying the program.

READING SKILLS

The Headline: The word *outlaw* is an old-fashioned term to describe a criminal, and it is commonly used to describe criminals in American western movies. Ask students to speculate why this word was used in the headline.

Making Inferences: Ask students what they think the reaction to the Iowa law is, judging from the article and the headline. Ask them what they think the journalist's attitude is. Have them support their conclusions with evidence from the article. (The journalist seems to quote more people who found the law useless or who are unenthusiastic about the law than those who think the law is useful.)

WORD STUDY

Suffixes: Point out the *-n* ending on *Iowa* to form the word *Iowan* (paragraph 3). The ending *-n*, *-an* or *-ian* is added to many place words to mean a native of a certain city, state or country. For example, people from Chicago are Chicagoans. People from California are Californians. People from Russia are Russians. Have students list more place names to which *-n*, *-an* or *-ian* is added for the name of inhabitants. Point out other suffixes commonly used to form words to describe people who live in a place (*-er*, *-ese*).

Slang: Point out the use of some common slang in the article: *kids* (paragraph 10) to mean children and teenagers; *cops* (paragraph 12) to mean police officers.

Synonyms: Have students list the words used to describe teenagers in the article: *anyone under 18, underaged offender, minors, juvenile, kids*. Point out that the words *minor* and *juvenile* are used in contexts relating to the law.

GRAMMAR AND SENTENCE PATTERNS

Parallel Structure: Point out the parallel structure of the verbs (could be) *fined, yanked* and *taken* in the long sentence that makes up paragraph 2. Mention that the use of three items in a series is a common rhetorical pattern in English. Have students practice parallel construction by completing sentences like these:

Smoking is _____, _____ and _____. (Use three parallel adjectives.)

In enforcing the law, the police have the option to _____, _____ and ______.

STYLE AND TONE

Conversational Tone: Since the article contains so many direct quotations, word choices are casual and conversational, and sentences are brief. The practice of using direct quotations is common in newspaper articles. It is a way for the journalist to present a variety of viewpoints. And, of course, interviews are often filled with quotations. To bring home this point, have students locate a newspaper article with several quotations and analyze what each quotation contributes to the main idea of the article. Also have them analyze if the tone of the quotations is conversational or more formal.

EXTENDED ACTIVITIES

Antismoking Movie: Obtain an antismoking movie or video from a library or from a health awareness group. Show it in class. Have a debate in your class about the new law or about other issues involved in smoking that the movie or video raises.

Letter Writing: Have students write a letter to the editor of a newspaper about an issue related to smoking; for example, the establishment of nonsmoking restaurants.

News: Article 2

Should ID's Be Required? Dutch Agonize

BACKGROUND

The need for the national ID in the Netherlands has been triggered by recent events in the European Community, which have seen a trend toward greater economic and political unity.

History of the European Community: In 1957, the Treaties of Rome created the European Economic Community (EEC). Its original members were Belgium, France, the German Federal Republic, Italy, Luxembourg and the Netherlands, and its mission was to ensure cooperation in agriculture, transportation and movement of capital and labor among the countries. Britain joined the community only in 1973, the same year that Denmark and Ireland became member nations. 1981 saw the entry of Greece, and 1986 that of Spain and Portugal. The actual European Community (EC) began in 1967 with the merger of the EEC with several other European institutions. The new organization had economic and political integration as its commitment. In 1987, another significant event occurred, the ratification of the Single European Act. This act set a deadline of December 31, 1992, to end all economic barriers and achieve a unified market, which would be the largest market in the world. In 1991, the Maastricht Treaty proposed an even greater unification, with one European foreign policy and the eventual establishment of a common European currency. However, the movement toward unification has met with obstacles on both the economic and political fronts, and the eventual pace toward achieving integration remains uncertain.

Issue of ID Cards: With the breaking down of intra-European barriers, the need for some sort of identification card for individuals to prove EC status has arisen. There is an EC passport, but for people who do not want to travel outside of the EC, the identification card would be a substitute. It seems likely that the Netherlands will adopt an ID card to fill this need. The issue of establishing a national ID is also a current one in Britain. Currently Belgium, West Germany, Greece, Luxembourg and Spain have mandatory IDs, and France, Italy and Portugal have voluntary ones. (The United States does not have a national ID card, although the Social Security card is in effect required for securing employment.)

As the article points out, people concerned with individual rights oppose a national ID. They feel that it could be a step toward totalitarianism, in which the government can exercise complete control over individuals' actions. Some people resent the potential intrusion on their privacy, since their actions can be tracked by means of the card.

However, as the article also points out, the ID has several positive points from the government's viewpoint: the card can be used to ensure that all workers pay taxes by requiring them to show their card on being employed. And it can be used to help identify people who disturb the peace, such as those who may provoke violence at sports events. In addition, standardized identification could have benefits for the citizens: it could help reduce fraud from use of false identification and ensure correct identification for recipients of welfare and entitlement programs.

Other Cards: The use of all types of cards is becoming increasingly common. For example, 82 percent of Americans have credit cards and use them for 10 percent of their purchases. Bank cards, such as ATM cards, allow people to get instant cash. More and more businesses have employee ID cards, which usually ensure that entrance to offices is restricted. And more and more people carry cards that give their medical profiles, which could save their lives in the case of an emergency.

RELATED READINGS

Articles in the Text: Another article that deals with the EC is the next article: "EC Sets 'Ecolabel' for Green Products."

Items in the News: As the member nations in the European Community seek to change their economic and political relationships with one another, there will be many stories about the EC in the news. Students who are interested can trace the most current events in this developing news story.

AUDIOVISUAL AIDS

Show students a map of Europe. Point out the Netherlands and the other EC member nations.

- The article is recorded on the audiocassettes accompanying the program.

READING SKILLS

Scanning: Have students scan the article for the following information:

1. What are the only EC countries that do not have identity cards? (paragraph 7)
2. How many people are believed to be working in the Netherlands illegally? (paragraph 13)
3. What does nearly everyone in the work force in the Netherlands have? (paragraph 15)

WORD STUDY

Negative Prefixes: Have students find the three negative prefixes in the article: *incompatible* (paragraph 2), *illegal* (paragraph 12), *unreported* (paragraph 13).

Adjective Forms: Many adjectives end in the suffixes *-al* or *-ic*. Several examples of these are in paragraph 3: *economic, judicial, political.* Have students identify the related noun (*economy, judge, politics*). Next have students find two other examples in the article: *traditional/tradition, democratic/democrat* (paragraph 2); *national/nation* (paragraph 5). Finally have students list other such related adjective/noun forms that they can think of. Other examples: *criminal/crime, governmental/government.*

GRAMMAR AND SENTENCE PATTERNS

The Verb Substitute *So*: The word *so* can be used to substitute for a verb so that the verb doesn't have to be repeated. The first two sentences in the article illustrate this use.

The French have one. So do the Germans and Belgians.

The *so* stands for *have one.* Note the inversion: the subject, *Germans and Belgians*, comes after the verb. Have students practice making sentences with *so*, using personal information. For example, Tina has a credit card, and so does Leo. Peter studies engineering, and so do Elaine and Michelle.

The Conjunction *So*: The word *so* can also be used as a conjunction expressing result. Point out the example in paragraph 15. Then have students complete these sentences based on the article and form similar ones of their own:

Many people think that an identity card is against the country's democratic values, so _____.

Police cannot identify people they arrest for minor crimes, so _____.

NUMBERS AND MEASUREMENTS

In oral reading, decimal points are often read as the word "point." For example, $5.8 million (paragraph 10) can be read as "five point eight million dollars." Another way to pronounce 5.8 is "five and eight tenths."

EXTENDED ACTIVITIES

Debate: Have students debate an issue in the news. Have them formulate their question in the *should* form: *Should . . . ?* Divide the class into two groups to support each side of the question.

News: Article 3

EC Sets 'Ecolabel' for Green Products

BACKGROUND

Ecology is a relatively new term. It refers to the study of the relationship of living things with their environment. In 1962, the term suddenly caught the attention of the world when Rachel Carson published her startling book *Silent Spring*. It described the horrors that humans were inflicting upon themselves and other living things by the use of massive amounts of insecticides and other chemicals that were sprayed into the atmosphere. Carson described how minute concentrations of chemicals entered the lakes and rivers, were absorbed by microscopic plants that were in turn eaten by tiny forms of life that then became food for fish, birds and larger animals. The farther up in the food chain, the larger was the concentration of chemicals. Many people came to realize that their water was unfit to drink and that the fish and beef they were eating often contained high levels of harmful chemicals.

Since 1962, environmental problems have become even more severe because of increased air pollution (from automobile exhausts and factory smoke) and increased water pollution (nuclear and industrial waste dumped into lakes, rivers and oceans). Another problem is the disposal of garbage. Garbage dumps or landfills were established. But as more and more garbage piled up, it became evident that in a short time, there would be no place to put it. In the U.S., laws were passed forbidding the dumping of toxic or nuclear wastes anywhere but at carefully controlled and licensed dump sites; the wastes must be sealed in approved containers that do not allow the contents to leak into the ground or water.

Over time, people have become more aware of the damage to the environment caused by the manufacture, use and disposal of items in daily use. For example, plastics that don't deteriorate create a disposal problem since they remain stored indefinitely in landfills. In recent years, many manufacturers have begun to package their products in containers that do not harm the environment. Such products are sought out by consumers who want to prevent environmental problems. It is, therefore, advantageous to manufacturers to be able to advertise that their product is environmentally safe. However, relying only on advertising, the consumer is sometimes misinformed as to whether a product is harmful or not. The ecolabel described in the article provides an objective standard that consumers can rely on.

Explanation of Terms:

spurious claims of ecological benevolence: This phrase, used in paragraph 4, refers to false or misleading advertising that suggests a product isn't harmful to the environment.

cradle-to-grave: This expression (in paragraph 6) means from birth to death. In the context of the article, it means from the time the product is manufactured until it is disposed of. A cradle-to-grave assessment analyzes the effect of the product in each stage of its life. How much energy is used to produce it? What by-products are created in its manufacturing, and how are they disposed of? Does its use harm the environment? And, finally, when it is discarded, will it naturally deteriorate over a short period of time without creating toxic chemicals or fumes in the process?

biodegradability: This term (used in paragraph 9) refers to the breakdown of material after it has been discarded. Food products, for example, are biodegradable because they decompose within a short time and can be absorbed into the environment without harm. Many plastics, on the other hand, are almost indestructible and remain intact for many years, creating serious waste disposal problems.

RELATED READINGS

Articles in the Text: The first article in the Science and Environment section deals with the problem of endangered species, another harmful result of our abuse of the environment. The two readings would be especially timely around Earth Day (on April 22) and World Environment Day (sponsored by the UN on June 5).

Additional Readings: Rachel Carson's *Silent Spring* (Boston: Houghton Mifflin, 1962) was the history-making best-seller that first alerted the world to the problems of pollution. It is highly recommended.

Environmental Organizations: The following organizations crusade on behalf of the environment and print materials about ecological problems and solutions. For further information, write to:

Greenpeace Action	Sierra Club
1436 U St. NW Suite 201-A	730 Polk Street
Washington, DC 20009	San Francisco, CA 94109

AUDIOVISUAL AIDS

A short film or videotape about ecology would help to emphasize the importance of the ecolabel and other efforts to save the environment.

- The article is recorded on the audiocassettes accompanying the program.

READING SKILLS

Scanning: Have students scan paragraphs 2, 10 and 11 to find out why this article is in the newspaper this week. In other words, why is this timely? What makes it a news story?

Main Ideas: Have students reread the article and make two lists: (1) ways that the ecolabel will help consumers and (2) ways that the ecolabel will help businesses (better than a variety of national labels would).

Making Inferences: Have students reread paragraph 3. What inference can be made from this paragraph? (You can use this question as a clue: Can a particular product always be made totally harmless to the environment?)

WORD STUDY

Word Meanings: Paragraph 4 contains several difficult words. Have students simplify the sentence by restating it using more familiar vocabulary. Ask students: In what two ways can consumers be misled? Simple answers might be: (1) by companies that make false claims that their products won't harm the environment; (2) by so many green labels (from different countries) that consumers get confused.

Irregular Plural: In paragraph 9, the word *criteria* is used. That is an irregular plural form. (The singular is *criterion.*) Have students look the word up in a dictionary to find its meaning and origin. Then ask them what *criteria* teachers use in giving students grades and what *criteria* people use when buying a car.

GRAMMAR AND SENTENCE PATTERNS

Markers of the Future: This reading is mostly about a new label that will be produced in the future. Have students underline everything in the article (verb forms, adverbs and time expressions) that convey the idea that the ecolabel is coming in the future. Discuss some of these different forms: future tense, active voice (paragraphs 1, 3 and so on); future tense, passive voice (paragraphs 6 and 10). Note that, in paragraph 10, *are to be joined* means "will be joined." Ask students who the doer of the action is in that sentence. (Who is doing the joining?) Also point out the use of *are expected to* in paragraph 11, another indication of future action.

EXTENDED ACTIVITIES

Student Discussion: Ask each student to come to class prepared to talk for one minute about an ecological problem and its possible solution. For example, a student can talk about auto emissions and mention as a possible solution an increased use of electric cars. Some topics you can suggest are industrial waste, acid rain, nuclear waste, rain forest destruction, endangered species, nonbiodegradable materials, global warming, noise pollution, insecticides, toxic waste dumps, smog (a combination of smoke and fog) and oil spills.

Guest Speaker: Look for a local organization that is willing to send a speaker to your classroom to discuss what individuals and school groups can do to maintain a healthy environment.

Recycling Project: If there is no recycling of paper and/or aluminum cans at your school, encourage students to organize a group to establish recycling.

News: Article 4

A Rain of Protest on Columbus's Parade

BACKGROUND

When we speak of a global economy today, we think of companies setting up bases of operations around the world. But as early as the 1400s, European explorers were looking for routes to the Orient, for them a land of spices and exotic goods. The most famous of these explorers was Columbus. In a broad sense, Columbus's voyage resembled another modern economic trend: it was a joint venture, a term sometimes used in business to describe cooperation among several nations on a business project. Columbus, who was born in Italy in 1451 and who had spent much of his life as a businessman and sailor in Portugal, got financing from King Ferdinand and Queen Isabella of Spain to sail on his now famous voyage.

Getting the backing for his voyage was not easy for Columbus. It took seven years of petitioning at courts before he was given permission to lead a group of sailors aboard three ships, the *Niña, Pinta* and *Santa Maria*. By following the maps of his time, he hoped to sail by way of the Canary Islands to China and India. Of course, the course led him instead to the Bahamas and Cuba. This was the first of several voyages that Columbus made to "the New World," where he established the first European town in America, called La Isabela, in the interior of Hispaniola (an island in the Caribbean now divided between Haiti and the Dominican Republic).

The Italian explorer, whose voyage five hundred years ago is celebrated with a national holiday in the United States, died in 1506 in Seville, Spain. His bones were shipped to Santo Domingo, then Havana, and then back to Seville in 1899. By the way, Columbus died in virtual poverty. Having proven a better explorer than administrator, he returned from his second voyage to Hispaniola in chains, after a rebellion in the colony. At the time of his death, he was still trying to recover his reputation at court.

The questioning of national observances like Columbus Day in the United States is part of a growing campaign of ethnic, racial and gender awareness called multiculturalism. American history is currently being reevaluated by some with the idea that it is composed of many stories, not one unified account. Indians, African-Americans, Hispanics, Asian-Americans and women are looking at key events and reinterpreting their importance. Perhaps this reevaluation will lead to more sensitivity in teaching about the contributions of minority groups to the American story. Others, however, say that forces such as the anti-Columbus Day group in Denver don't properly honor the country's traditional heroes and that their demonstrations will lead to discord and confusion.

RELATED READINGS

Items in the News: Have students clip items in the news pertaining to the celebration of Columbus's voyage or to other national celebrations and bring them to class to discuss or display. Alternately, you can have students look for examples of issues in the news that relate to the conflict or tensions among ethnic groups in a country. Have students discuss the issues the articles raise.

AUDIOVISUAL AIDS

Maps from Columbus's time and current maps can be found in encyclopedias or in history books and used to show the background of the story of Columbus. Places that are associated with Columbus in Europe (Genoa, Portugal, Castile and Seville) and the Americas can be pointed out on the current world maps.

- The article is recorded on the audiocassettes accompanying the program.

READING SKILLS

Use of the Colon: In paragraph 2, notice the use of the colon (:) in the first sentence to introduce a clause beginning with *that.* The colon is sometimes used as a stylistic device to relate two ideas, often to signal the movement from a general statement to a specific clarification. Ask students to explain the two related ideas (the obvious/civilization began before the arrival of the Europeans). The use here is somewhat unconventional; usually the element following the colon is a complete sentence, not a clause.

Use of Dashes with Appositives: In paragraph 13, notice that a dash is used to separate an appositive (a noun or group of nouns that describes the preceding noun) from the rest of the sentence. A comma (,) before and after the appositive is generally used to perform this function, but a dash is sometimes used, as in this example. The dash suggests a stronger break, or it may be used when the use of many commas in a string would be confusing. Here is a sentence containing another appositive:

> The article describes two groups in conflict over a holiday—*Italian Americans and Native Americans.*

Using the sentence as a model, have students write two sentences with appositives, one with commas and one with dashes.

WORD STUDY

Compound Words: Notice the hyphenated words in paragraphs 4 and 5, *Italian-Americans* and *African-Americans.* This is the way that Americans identify their ethnic origins. Point out that it is not uncommon to see the compounds without hyphens. Notice that Native Americans (meaning Indians) in paragraph 10 is not hyphenated (it is composed of adjective and noun, not two nouns).

GRAMMAR AND SENTENCE PATTERNS

Appositives and Relative Clauses: Have students find appositives (see Reading Skills) and relative clauses (*who, which* and *that* clauses) in the article. You can begin with the first sentence about Will Rogers. Notice that appositives and relative clauses often identify people (paragraphs 5, 9 and 12, for instance): *Mayor Wellington Webb, who is black,* . . . You might also have students practice turning relative clauses into appositives where possible (by removing *who, which* and *that* plus the verb *be*).

Wellington Webb, *who is the mayor of Denver,* is being asked to remove a plaque honoring Columbus. (clause)

Wellington Webb, *the mayor of Denver,* is being asked to remove a plaque honoring Columbus. (appositive)

(Remove *who is* and point out the resulting appositive.)

NUMBERS AND MEASUREMENTS

Point out to students how *th* is added to the number 500 when it is used as an ordinal number (designating a number in a sequence): the 500th anniversary of the voyage. Common uses of ordinal numbers are for calendar dates (October 12th), floors of a building (the 15th floor), and grades in school (6th grade). Have students write a few sentences using ordinal numbers.

EXTENDED ACTIVITIES

Presentation: Have students use an encyclopedia to look up the voyage of another famous explorer. Have them present their information orally in a brief paragraph. Suggest that they refer to a map as they make their presentation. Let the other students guess the name of the explorer. If you want to extend the game further, have the other students interview the "explorer," using the common question words: *who, what, where, when, why* and *how.*

Heroes: Have students write a paragraph about a person who they think is a hero and tell why. Have students share their responses with the class.

SECTION 2: OPINION

Opinion: Article 1

You Can't Learn Soccer in the Suburbs

BACKGROUND

As the author of the article states, soccer is the most popular sport in the world. Organized soccer has 20 million players participating in 150 nations on nearly every continent. The World Cup of Soccer, held every four years, is watched by a billion viewers. Some of the larger soccer stadiums, such as one in Brazil, can hold 200,000 fans.

Known as "football" in many nations, soccer's simple rules evolved from centuries of different ball games. Formal rules, such as those that allow only the goalie to touch the ball with his or her hands did not develop until late in the nineteenth century. Rugby and U.S.-style football developed even later.

Nearly 9 million young people play soccer in the United States. The game is played at colleges and universities and is equally popular among young men and women. In American youth leagues, nearly 40 percent of the soccer competitors are girls. However, as a professional sport, soccer is not very popular in the U.S., and professional leagues have not had much consistent success in the face of other sports, such as baseball, U.S-style football and basketball.

Although interest in soccer has grown in the United States, it is in Europe and Latin America that soccer enjoys the largest following. In professional competition every four years, about one hundred national teams play for the World Cup. Soccer is also an Olympic sport.

Explanation of Terms:
The author mentions these terms that were in the news.

contras: Nicaraguan counter-revolutionaries

Eastern Airlines: Now out-of-business U.S. commercial passenger airline

perestroika: Name for economic and social reform in the Soviet Union before the fall of communism

Ricky Villa, Platini, Pelé: Famous professional soccer players

RELATED READINGS

Articles in the Text: Students might discuss how culture is imported and exported: soccer in the United States, Disney in France ("Is There a European Accent in Euro Disneyland?" in Arts and Leisure); French cooks in Moscow ("Moscow Chefs: Where's the Beef?" in Education); baseball in Paris ("In Europe, It's Still Diamonds in the Rough" in Sports); basketball shoes around the world ("King of the Court: High-Tech, High-Price Sneakers" in Business). Many of the articles in the book deal with these cultural exchanges.

Items in the News: Have students clip items in the news about soccer and bring them to class for discussion.

AUDIOVISUAL AIDS

Obtain a sports video showing highlights of soccer games and show it in class. You might also bring in articles, photos or films of great soccer players such as Pelé.

- The article is recorded on the audiocassettes accompanying the program.

READING SKILLS

Making Inferences:

- Ask students: What can you guess about soccer in the U.S. from the information presented in the article? Possible responses: It is not often televised on nonpay TV. It is popular among young people who live in the suburbs. Most Americans do not understand or appreciate soccer.

- Ask students to speculate on what has led the author to his views about soccer in the United States. Is the author really making a complaint about U.S. soccer or giving a personal reaction to how things have changed since his youth? Also, students might discuss the thoroughness of the author's evidence. Might soccer be played in less affluent areas of the United States? Might immigrants from soccer-playing countries be participating in urban experiences of soccer? Why couldn't the author include these possibilities in his discussion?

WORD STUDY

American vs. British English: The British writer uses certain words in the article that are more common in British than American English. Notice that in paragraph 6, the author refers to his mother as my "mum." Americans would say "mom." Have students think of other differences between British and American English, such as *telly* vs. *TV, lift* vs. *elevator, queue* vs. *line*.

Compound Words: Notice the use of hyphenated words like *right-thinking* (paragraph 1), *dope-ridden* (paragraph 4), *hype-laden* (paragraph 6). Point out that these hyphenated words form compounds used to describe nouns. Note that in these compounds, the second word is a participle. Have students think of other compound words that follow this pattern of word + participle + modified noun. Have them look in other readings to find examples.

GRAMMAR AND SENTENCE PATTERNS

Intentional Sentence Fragments: A sentence, of course, contains a subject and verb. Sometimes writers choose to punctuate phrases or even single words as sentences. Fragments are usually to be avoided in English unless they are intended for emphasis, or under special conditions such as in answering questions or as exclamations. Have students find the sentence fragments in the article: *No choice.* (paragraph 1); *Pshaw!* (paragraph 5). Discuss with students why the author might have chosen to use these fragments.

STYLE AND TONE

Tone: An author's attitude toward material is expressed as tone. One can say that a writer is being humorous, serious, sarcastic, shrill, subdued and so on. Discuss how the writer establishes a humorous or ironic tone by comparing soccer stars Platini and Pelé with Gorbachev (paragraph 6) and by calling Ted Turner a global visionary (paragraph 1). Discuss how he uses a nostalgic tone in referring to his parents' relationship with the Liverpool Football Club Stadium (paragraph 6).

NUMBERS AND MEASUREMENTS

Notice that the full name of a year can be shortened by using an apostrophe: '66 for 1966; '81 for 1981 (paragraph 6).

EXTENDED ACTIVITIES

Survey: Conduct a survey among students about what sport is the most popular. Let them list the sport they most like to play and the sport they most like to observe. Are the two sports the same? Are there national differences?

Research Report: Have students do research on the history of a sport or on a famous soccer player. Have them present the research in class.

Opinion: Article 2

An Economics Lesson at the Barbershop

BACKGROUND

It is the editorial writer's opinion that a Japanese barbershop, where a customer is treated royally, is the perfect symbol of Japan's flourishing economy. He cites the attention to detail and the dedication to service offered by the owners as clues to what makes Japan, in general, "the envy of the capitalist world."

To evaluate the services offered at the barbershop from a Japanese point of view, it is important to stress the overcrowding of major Japanese cities, the heavy industrialization of the island republic and the many hours the Japanese spend at work. Perhaps to escape these conditions, the Japanese excel at creating beauty in their daily lives. Whether it's beautiful floral arrangements, miniature bonsai trees, artistically designed sushi or the small delicate poetic form haiku, the Japanese know how to create serenity and instant "escape." The hot towel and warm shaving cream treatment of the Tanakas' barbershop, then, falls easily into the category of small pleasures.

Another striking feature of Japanese society is its homogeneity. Although the island nation is spread out over the map, its culture is largely shared and its population is ethnically unified. The Tanakas needn't worry about creating a vast variety of different hairstyles. They can concentrate on doing an essential number well.

Also by Japanese standards, even the expanded version of the barbershop is small and intimate. The Japanese are used to shopping at huge department stores called *depato,* which sometimes house zoos, playgrounds, restaurants and art exhibits. The simplicity of the barbershop contrasts with the variety and pace of the department stores. By the way, the *depato* are often in commuter terminals.

RELATED READINGS

Articles in the Text: The articles on Japanese culture in the text might be taught as a unit. In addition to this article, students might read "Sociology of the Kimono: Everything Old Is Young" (Business section), "For Japanese, Cramming for Exams Starts Where the Cradle Leaves Off" (Education section) and "Hey, Give Yourself a Break and Go Jump in a Hole" (Arts and Leisure section).

Items in the News: Feature articles in the newspaper often describe how things are done differently in a different culture. Have students choose a culture and find articles on it. Have students discuss how the culture is presented in the news. What assumptions about the culture are usually made? What aspects about the culture are usually stressed?

AUDIOVISUAL AIDS

- Bring in a map of Tokyo. Locate the area of the Tanakas' barbershop. Locate the Ginza district. In addition, bring in photos of Japan or items from traditional Japanese culture including kimonos, bonsai trees, food and so on.
- Have students watch a video or film of some aspect of life in modern Japan.

- The article is recorded on the audiocassettes accompanying the program.

READING SKILLS

Chronological Order/Process: Have the students list, step by step, the process in which the customer takes part from the moment of entering the Tanakas' barbershop until the end of the visit.

WORD STUDY

Specialized Vocabulary: Students should know the parts of the body and hair referred to in the article. They include *scalp* (paragraph 10); *sideburns* (paragraph 11); *whisker, forehead* and *earlobes* (paragraph 13).

Derivations: Discuss these derivations with your students: *sideburns* (an alteration of burnsides, from Ambrose E. Burnside, an American Civil War commander, who wore heavy side whiskers); and *whiskers* (from whisk, a small bunch of twigs or hair).

Syllabication and Phonics: Point out that in words with double consonants (like *assume* in paragraph 4, *possible* in paragraph 5, and *better* in paragraph 6), the syllable division is between consonants: as/sume, pos/si/ble, bet/ter. This is true of all words in English unless the double consonant is at the end of the word. Point out that even though the consonant is doubled in the spelling, there is only one consonant sound.

STYLE AND TONE

Because this article praises Japanese barbershops, many of the words chosen exaggerate their positive qualities. Have students discuss this use of exaggeration (or hyperbole) in word choice by looking at the following words: *odyssey* and *miracle* (paragraph 2), *honorific stature* (paragraph 4), *showstopper* (paragraph 12).

EXTENDED ACTIVITIES

Research Report: Have students research a typical Japanese business institution and report on it.

Services: If any students in class have ever visited a Japanese barbershop, have them report on their experience. Alternately, they could write about a service or a way of doing things that they have experienced in a different culture that contrasts with a service from their native culture.

Opinion: Article 3

Much Ado About Mozart: Craze Leaves Expert 'Astounded'

BACKGROUND

This article discusses the commemoration of the death of Wolfgang Amadeus Mozart, who was born on January 27, 1756, in Salzburg, Austria, and died on December 5, 1791. As most people know, Mozart was a musical prodigy, but what were his accomplishments at an early age? By age 4, he could play the harpsichord, by 5 he was composing music, and at the tender age of 6, he had already played for the court in Vienna.

His early musical talent was nurtured by his father, a musician and leader of the local orchestra. Mozart never studied formally at school but continued under the tutorship of his father to develop his profound talents. By age 14, he had written many sonatas and had toured Europe, giving performances.

After working for more than 10 years under the sponsorship of the archbishop of Salzburg, Mozart quarreled with him in 1781 and was dismissed. He settled in Vienna, where he tried to make a living by selling his works. Despite his prolific musical output, which included symphonies, church music, concertos, chamber music and many operas, he died in poverty in 1791.

Although Mozart's later life was difficult, his music is full of vigor and cheerfulness. He was known to have a wonderful sense of humor, which is reflected in several of his light operas, such as *Così fan tutte* (All Women Are Like That) and *Le nozze di Figaro* (The Marriage of Figaro). *Don Giovanni* and *The Magic Flute*, operas composed late in his career, the first in Italian and the second in German, display the range of Mozart's talent from comedy to tragedy. Along with Joseph Haydn, he is remembered as a leading composer of the classical period, making many innovations that affected the future of music.

Elements of Mozart's biography, such as his early talent and tragically premature death, have led to more interest in Mozart than in Haydn, however. Not only is there a yearly festival in Mozart's native Salzburg to commemorate his music, but Lincoln Center in New York City also sponsors the "Mostly Mozart Festival" every summer. As the article states, the successful adaptation of Peter Shaffer's play "Amadeus" to the screen by director Milos Forman has created a swell of interest in this talented musician. The interview about Mozart explores the issue of his celebrity status against the pure power of his music.

RELATED READINGS

Articles in the Text: Have students read "A Rain of Protest on Columbus's Parade." It is clear by examining that article and this one on Mozart that the reputations of historical figures undergo constant revision. Have students discuss this issue and think of other examples of famous people whose reputations have risen or fallen over time.

AUDIOVISUAL AIDS

- Show the movie "Amadeus" to the class and discuss the image of Mozart as presented in the movie.
- Bring videotapes of any of Mozart's operas to class, or have students listen to recordings of Mozart's music and discuss their reactions.
- The article is recorded on the audiocassettes accompanying the program.

READING SKILLS

Contrasting Information: As students read the Mozart article, have them keep track of the facts vs. myths about Mozart. Ask them to look for at least two facts and two myths as they read. Students might also be asked to look for contrasts between Mozart and Haydn contained in the article.

WORD STUDY

Synonyms: Have students compare similar words contained in the article:

fuss (paragraph 1)/ *craze* (paragraph 5)/ *phenomenon* (paragraph 6)
amazing (paragraph 4)/ *taken by surprise* (paragraph 5)/ *astounded* (paragraph 6)
appeals (paragraph 2)/ *attracts* (paragraph 4)

Abbreviations: CD (paragraph 8) is defined within the article. Students might want to discuss other recent abbreviations that refer to advances in technology, like PC (personal computer). How many of them still own LPs (long-playing records, which have largely been replaced by CDs)? Can they think of other recent abbreviations?

GRAMMAR AND SENTENCE PATTERNS

Questions: Have students pay particular attention to the sentence structure of the questions within the interview. They should notice the inverted verb/subject word order, which is typical of interrogative sentences. Students should also notice that a number of questions are really declarative sentences punctuated as questions. In an interview, these sentences would be taken as questions because the speaker would say them with his or her voice rising toward the end of the sentence. Demonstrate this technique with the following sentence:

He appeals a lot to young people? (paragraph 3).

Ask students how the sentence might be rewritten in interrogative form: Does he appeal . . .?

STYLE AND TONE

Interview Pattern: Discuss the interview pattern further. Students might be asked to rewrite part of the article by removing the questions and making the answers coherent without them. What changes must be made to do so? (Topic sentences must be introduced into paragraphs.)

Colloquialisms: Point out that although the interview is for a newspaper article about a sophisticated arts topic, the language used is sometimes very colloquial: *You know what I think?* Nothing is going to happen. (paragraph 18); *an awful lot* (paragraph 20).

EXTENDED ACTIVITIES

Presentation: Have students in groups choose an opera or symphony by Mozart to study. They can bring in a CD or tape of the music and present their prepared research.

Guest Speaker: Have a classical music expert come to class and lecture further on Mozart and other composers of the period.

Interview: Have students interview other class members on topics about which they are "experts." The interviews could be done orally as a group activity or individually with students writing up the results of their interviews.

Opinion: Article 4

National Cliché or Good Metaphor?

BACKGROUND

While not all students reading this article will agree with the idea that entire nations can be characterized by a single metaphor, most would concede that one person's metaphor is another's cliché.

How fresh and how accurate we judge a phrase to be depends upon our familiarity with it. Americans have heard "sly as a fox" a hundred times. The phrase has therefore become a cliché. But a person from another culture, hearing the same phrase, might think it quite inventive. The person might also offer his or her language's version of it; for example, "crafty as a monkey."

While traveling on business, an American might need to go to his or her hotel room "and sleep on it" before making a decision. Meanwhile, a Spanish counterpart is "consulting one's pillow" (*consultar con la almobada*) before reaching a conclusion. In Italy, the American tourist may notice that every "Tom, Dick and Harry" (familiar American names) is carrying a camera and guidebook. In Italy, those same familiar fellows are "Tizio, Caio e Sempronio."

It is obvious, then, that while each language presents a fresh solution to the problem of describing a situation or phenomenon, there are equivalent phrases in many languages. And whether the phrase strikes a listener as a metaphor or cliché depends upon his or her familiarity with it.

A further point of discussion for the Gannon article is whether or not national metaphors are merely stereotypes. Would all French citizens agree that they are perfectionists? Would Italians assent to their characterization as emotional just because they are from the country where opera had its development? In the United States, the common metaphor for its diverse people is a melting pot, in which a national character gets stirred, seasoned and blended. Would its diverse citizenry agree to the aggressive metaphor of football?

The problem with asserting that all of any group fits a pattern is that one can overgeneralize. "All women are X." "All men are Y." How true and useful are statements such as these? Can lace more than superficially explain the character of Belgians? Do fiestas adequately characterize the diversity of Mexican society? See what students think about the uses and dangers of making such sweeping generalizations.

RELATED READINGS

Articles in the Text: "Food for Luck" in the Arts and Leisure section surveys the symbolic meaning of food in a variety of cultures. It might be discussed in relation to this article. The issue of cultural diversity is explored in a number of articles (see Related Readings for the first article in this Opinion section, "You Can't Learn Soccer in the Suburbs").

Items in the News: Students might be alert to news and magazine articles that discuss the customs or habits of a culture. Can the practices described be seen as metaphors for the cultures? Clip articles and bring them to class for a discussion.

AUDIOVISUAL AIDS

Mexican fiestas, Spanish bullfights, French vineyards, German symphonies and so on—pictures from travel magazines or brochures might be brought to class so that each metaphor in the Gannon article gets connected to an image. In addition, travel posters that convey a culture in a single image or collage of images are sometimes available. These might also be brought to class for discussion: Do the images give insight into a culture or are they just stereotypes?

READING SKILLS

Making Inferences: Have students state how Gannon might summarize his work and its value, based on the information given in the article. Have students discuss the value of understanding how people's behavior is related to the society they belong to.

WORD STUDY

Suffixes: Notice how different word endings change the part of speech of the root word:

patient (adj.)/ patiently (adv.)
harmony (n.)/harmonious (adj.)
character (n.)/characterize (v.)
collect (v.)/collection (n.)

Stress to students the regularity with which these suffix endings change one part of speech to another. The suffix *-ly* is an adverb ending. The suffix *-(i)ous* is an adjective ending. The suffix *-ize* is a verb ending. The suffix *-(t)ion* is a noun ending. Using the following sets of words, have students list the root word and use both the root word and the suffixed word in sentences.

Adverbs: quietly, quickly, lightly, silently, endlessly
Adjectives: humorous, delirious
Verbs: visualize, theorize
Nouns: connection, inspection, rejection, selection

Academic Studies: Point out the two words that describe academic fields: *anthropologists, organizational theorists* (paragraph 8). Have students look in dictionaries and reference books to define the fields. Have them list all the other academic fields they can and define them (e.g., *physicist, biologist*).

GRAMMAR AND SENTENCE PATTERNS

Prepositional Phrases: Many English sentences contain prepositional phrases. Have students underline all the prepositional phrases in the first sentence of paragraph 13. They will find four: *to other cultures, with the metaphor, of the French vineyard, in mind.* With students, make a list of other common prepositions in English: *at, on, over, under, from, across, between, behind, before, after, during.*

EXTENDED ACTIVITIES

Cultural Views: Show a film or video that portrays a culture that Gannon discusses. After seeing the film or video, is the class more or less convinced by Gannon's claims?

Ethnic Items: Have students bring in items that they believe are useful in illustrating their native culture and explain their choices to the class.

Opinion: Article 5

Hold Your Nose at the Steak House

BACKGROUND

As this article makes clear, Jeremy Rifkin, an environmental activist and author, is an outspoken critic of the beef industry. He holds it responsible for pollution, global warming, world hunger and a high-fat, unhealthy diet for its consumers. His article suggests that beef-dependent countries such as the United States, the world's largest producer, need to decrease cattle production for the sake of our planet.

Despite the statistics that he cites, the beef culture has spread beyond the United States. Even countries such as Japan, which produce very little beef, now regard it as a desirable commodity. In the United States, where beef is "king," large cattle feedlots in the West may handle more than 20,000 head of cattle at a time. The average American eats 100 pounds of beef a year, which amounts to nearly 40 percent of his or her average protein intake. Outside of the United States, beef and veal (young cattle) production is 64 billion pounds a year.

Rifkin suggests that consumers limit their intake of beef for their own health and the sake of the environment. Doing so would reduce the destruction of the tropical rain forest and increase the amount of grain available for human consumption.

One alternative to beef that two million people in the United States now practice is vegetarianism. A vegetarian abstains from eating the flesh of any animal. This is an ancient diet regime traditionally tied to Eastern religions such as Buddhism, which stress the kinship of humans and animals. Recently, with a mind on the environment and a healthier, fat-free diet, the vegetarian regime has spread globally among more affluent eaters. Even the best restaurants in major American cities feature a gourmet vegetarian platter on their menus. And many who choose a steak for dinner now and then are bypassing the fast food counter and opting for healthier choices.

RELATED READINGS

Articles in the Text: Several other articles deal with food: "Moscow Chefs: Where's the Beef?" (Education section) and "Food for Luck" (Arts and Leisure section). These might be grouped together for discussion. "Smokers Under 18 in Iowa Now Outlaws" (News section) and the issue of smoking itself might be compared with the Rifkin article for a discussion of healthful and unhealthful habits.

Items in the News: Have students clip articles about beef consumption or articles on diet in general for a discussion in class.

AUDIOVISUAL AIDS

- See if you can find a video related to the beef industry and the consumption of beef to show in class. In addition, films about global warming, the destruction of the tropical rain forest and world hunger can also be shown.
- Students might be interested in nutritional charts recommending healthful foods. These might be available from government agencies. Current nutritional charts have deemphasized meat consumption in a balanced diet. Such charts might be compared to earlier versions that relied more on meat as a source of calories.

READING SKILLS

Main Ideas: Point out that paragraphs often have topic sentences that summarize the main point of the paragraph. The author of this article uses them to begin many paragraphs. Have the students locate some of these sentences (for example, the first sentences in paragraphs 5, 8, 11, 12, 15).

Evidence: Have students list all of the statistics used in the article to support one of the main ideas: that beef production damages the environment, that beef production leads to global hunger or that U.S. government policy toward beef consumption is wrong. Students might be told to underline these facts as a scanning exercise.

WORD STUDY

Dictionary Work: Have students look up the meaning of the following words pertaining to beef production and consumption: *steers, feed* (n.), *livestock, cud, marbling, saturated fat, lean* (adj.).

GRAMMAR AND SENTENCE PATTERNS

Passive Constructions: Read the second sentence in paragraph 3: "Entrance into the beef culture was viewed by many immigrants as a rite of passage into the middle class." This is a passive construction with the object (*entrance into the beef culture*) serving as the subject and the agent or doer (*immigrants*) in a prepositional phrase with *by*. Have students recast the sentence as an active construction and begin it with "Many immigrants have viewed. . . ." Have students look for other examples of the passive voice in the article: *were* *sold* (paragraph 1); *have been razed* (paragraph 5); *is being destroyed* (paragraph 6); *were converted* (paragraph 10); *is expected* (paragraph 11); *must be overhauled, was abandoned, should be restructured* (paragraph 15).

STYLE AND TONE

Figurative Language: Discuss the metaphor contained in the quotation in paragraph 3: "On the shoals of roast beef and apple pie, all socialist utopias founder." Have students use a dictionary if necessary to look up the meanings of the words *shoals* and *founder*. Then discuss the visual image suggested by it. Is it meant to evoke humor? What does it say about people's commitment to politics? to good food? Do students agree?

NUMBERS AND MEASUREMENTS

This article contains many measurements. Note that two systems are given: the metric and the U.S./British one. Compare pounds and kilograms (paragraph 1), gallons and liters (paragraph 7), ounces and grams (paragraph 7), and acres and hectares (paragraph 13). Students may want a ready-made chart of the measures and conversion formulas for moving from one system to the other. A chart of comparisons might be found in a dictionary or mathematics text.

EXTENDED ACTIVITIES

Diet Tracking: Ask students to keep a log of their food intake for a week. At the end of the week, have them count how many servings of beef they consumed.

Interview: Have students interview a vegetarian about his or her eating habits. What made this person adopt a vegetarian diet? Is it difficult to be a vegetarian in a meat-eating society?

SECTION 3: BUSINESS

Business: Article 1

Sociology of the Kimono: Everything Old is Young

BACKGROUND

For the Western reader, this article about the kimono may raise as many questions as it answers. The traditional Japanese kimono is a quite different garment from the kimono-style bathrobe popular in the West. The name itself does nothing to describe the garment. The word *kimono* means clothing, or literally a thing (*mono*) worn (*kiru*).

Paragraph 1 in the article raises one question that most Western readers will ask. Why does it take 20 minutes or more to get into a kimono? Part of the answer lies in the fact that women wear several layers of undergarments beneath the kimono. Second, keeping the kimono closed is not simply a matter of zipping or buttoning. In *The Kimono Mind*, Bernard Rudofsky quotes from a Japanese handbook that describes the step-by-step process of putting on a kimono:

> First, put on a white cotton vest and silk or cotton underskirt, then the white socks; next the undergarment is tied at the waist with a waist-tie just below the waist, and draw the extra length of material so that the hemline will just cover the heels. Fold this down over the tie. Then tie another waist-tie about and wind another undersash around the waist. Next tie the obi.

Once a narrow sash, the obi has evolved into a stiff wide band. It flattens out the woman's breasts, and it has been compared to the Western corset (or girdle). Getting the obi on just right is another long procedure. The handbook instructions continue as follows:

> Wind the obi around the waist twice. Tie the ends of the obi behind, holding the longer end above the knot and the shorter below. Tug tightly. Fold the longer end down over the obi-bustle wrapped in a bustle-sash and tie the ends of the latter in front, tucking the ends about the obi.

The instructions go on and on. There are many ways of tying the obi into decorative shapes in the back. It is sometimes a bustle, a bow or a hump. There may also be a board covered with fabric. The obi is secured by a small pillow, sashes and braided cord.

Paragraph 11 mentions some of the accessories to the kimono. The tabi (socks) have split toes and are generally white. The sandals worn with a kimono may be flat or up to four inches high.

Westerners may wonder how the kimono became standard for women, since it does very little to display the parts of the feminine figure. The style of the kimono makes more sense if one considers that, before the 19th century (when Japan's isolationism ended), the kimono was standard attire for *both* men and women. In fact, for many centuries, Japanese men and women dressed so much alike that it is difficult to identify the sex of the people in old Japanese prints. Today, the only remnant of the kimono's unisex origin is the *yukata*, the kimono-like cotton robes worn after a bath and at hot spring resorts and summer festivals. Both men and women wear these.

Many rules go along with the wearing of the kimono. The left side is always crossed over the right, except when dressing someone who has died. Unmarried women wear longer sleeves than married women do. In paragraph 13, the article talks about the color rules, some of which are being broken today. In the past, age, marital status and the season of the year all helped to determine the color of a woman's kimono. Younger women wore brighter colors, such as pink, red and orange. Older women wore paler colors, such as lavender. Today, if a man wears a kimono, it is usually black, gray or brown. But most Japanese men wear Western clothing except on special occasions.

RELATED READINGS

Articles in the Text: This is the second of four articles about Japan in the text. The others are in these sections: Opinion, Education, and Arts and Leisure.

Additional Readings: For a general survey of Japanese life, the following references are excellent:

Perkins, Dorothy. *Encyclopedia of Japan: Japanese History from Abacus to Zori.* New York: A Roundtable Press Book, 1991.

Lands and Peoples: Asia, Australia, New Zealand, Oceania. Volume 2. Danbury, CT: Grolier, Inc., 1989.

Two books that give detailed information about the kimono and many insights into Japanese culture are the following:

Rudofsky, Bernard. *The Kimono Mind: An Informal Guide to Japan and the Japanese.* Garden City, NY: Doubleday, 1965.

Yamanaka, Norio. *The Book of Kimono.* Tokyo and New York: Harper and Row, 1982.

AUDIOVISUAL AIDS

The best possible visual aid would, of course, be a real Japanese kimono. In addition or as a substitute, Japanese prints with drawings of people wearing kimonos can also be shown. Students should be able to see changes in the kimono over the centuries and how it developed from a soft, flowing gown that clung to the body into a more geometric and rigid style.

READING SKILLS

Fact vs. Opinion: In paragraph 9, a Japanese designer says, "Being fashionable is being different from others." Is that statement fact or opinion? Students can discuss their reactions.

Comparisons: Have students make a chart to compare Sueko Otsuka's kimono with that of Wada.

WORD STUDY

Color Words: Paragraph 13 contains some color words, so this is a good time to practice these. Name the colors that appear in the students' clothing. (Look for *maroon,* mentioned in paragraph 13). Also, name common patterns (plaid, stripes, dots and so on) used in clothing. Have students practice the color vocabulary by describing clothing worn by people in pictures that you show them.

Words and Phrases about Business: Have students define and discuss the following words about business:

brand name, retail and wholesale, produce and manufacture, market and consumer

Pronunciation: Nouns ending in *-tion* are usually stressed on the next-to-last syllable. Have students pronounce (and then define) the following verb-noun pairs. Point out the stress change.

eliminate / elimination	preserve / preservation
imitate / imitation	preoccupy / preoccupation
innovate / innovation	

Word Parts:

- The words *garment* and *undergarment* appear in the article. Define these, and ask students to name other compound words beginning with *under*.
- Discuss the meaning of *-wide*, as in *nationwide* and *worldwide*.

GRAMMAR AND SENTENCE PATTERNS

Adjective Study: Students can make a list of all the adjectives they find that describe the kimono (*austere, unique, geometric, expensive, traditional* and so on). This can be done as a game, with partners competing to create the longest list.

Irregular Verbs: Discuss the meanings and forms of the irregular verbs *shrink* (paragraph 16) and *split* (paragraph 17).

EXTENDED ACTIVITIES

Poetry Study: Students will enjoy reading some *haikus* (short Japanese poems) and then trying to write their own.

Ethnic Items: Encourage students to show and explain some traditional items from their native countries.

Business: Article 2

For Eskimo Artists Seeking Inspiration, Money Talks

BACKGROUND

Eskimos are native inhabitants of the Arctic and sub-Arctic regions of North America and the northeastern tip of Siberia. Their homeland stretches from Siberia across Alaska, northern Canada and Greenland, spanning four countries. Today, there are about 120,000 Eskimos in all four regions. About 23,000 of these live in Canada.

Actually, the word *Eskimo* did not come from the language of the people who are commonly called Eskimos today. It came from an American Indian (Native American) word meaning eaters of raw meat. To identify themselves, Eskimos use various words that can be translated as "people" or "real people." Canadian Eskimos call themselves *Inuit* or *Inuvialit*; Alaskan Eskimos use the term *Yupik* or *Inupiat*; Siberian Eskimos are *Yupik* or *Yuit*. However, in recent years, some have also begun to use the word *Eskimo*.

For thousands of years, Eskimos lived near the sea. Their food, clothing and other needs were met by the animals that lived in the area. They caught fish and hunted seals, walruses, whales, polar bears and caribou (a kind of deer). These animals, so important to their survival, also became the main subjects of their art.

During the long history of Eskimo culture, Eskimos usually produced art for a purpose, either religious or utilitarian. They made amulets to scare off evil spirits. They carved wooden masks for ceremonial dances. They made baskets and spears for everyday use. They often decorated the things they had made for practical use. For example, they trimmed their clothing with fur, ivory buttons and fancy buckles carved in the shape of seals. They decorated their tools by making etchings on them. They carved children's toys of bone and ivory.

The animistic Eskimo religion imputed spirits (souls) to animals and important features of the landscape. The Eskimos believed that human beings had several souls. One of these was associated with the individual's name. When a baby was named after someone who had died, the Eskimos believed that the dead person's soul was then transferred to the newborn.

When Europeans began arriving in the mid-1700s, the life of the Eskimos began to change. In the 1800s, a great many European whalers and fur traders came to the Far North. The Eskimos sailed with the whalers and hunted with the fur traders. As a result, many of the animals that Eskimos needed to sustain their traditional way of life were almost totally destroyed. New scientific and religious ideas took hold in the Eskimo community, and Eskimo art gradually came to reflect the demands of a new souvenir market. Thus, the influence of outside cultures upon Eskimo art was not a sudden development, but a gradual one. Today's Eskimos are greatly influenced by the dominant culture in which they live. Traditional foods, clothing and housing styles have often been replaced by more contemporary items. Canada still has isolated areas where Eskimos are involved in traditional hunting and trapping. But most Canadian Eskimos now live in towns and settlements with modern facilities.

Some Eskimos live farther north than any other people, in an area with a very cold, harsh climate. The region is commonly called the land of the midnight sun because, for a portion of the summer, it has 24 hours of daylight. However, for part of each winter, there is no sunlight at all. The long winters bring temperatures averaging between -20 degrees F (-29 degrees C) to -30 degrees F (-34 degrees C).

Northwest Territories: The dateline of this article is Northwest Territories (NWT). This region of Canada includes all of mainland Canada that is north of 60 degrees north latitude between the Yukon Territory on the west and Hudson Bay on the east. It also includes all the islands between the mainland and the North Pole.

In fact, the NWT accounts for one third of all Canadian land. This large area is quite thinly populated. It covers 1,322,909 square miles (3,426,320 square kilometers), but has a population of only about 53,000.

RELATED READINGS

Additional Readings: One text with many beautiful illustrations of Eskimo arts and crafts is: Ray, Dorothy Jean. *Aleut and Eskimo Art: Tradition and Innovation in South Alaska.* Seattle, WA: University of Washington Press, 1981.

Although this text is not about Canadian Eskimos, it shows artwork that is very similar to that of the Canadian Eskimos.

AUDIOVISUAL AIDS

Show photographs of some of the animals that Eskimos often use in their art (seals, whales and so on). Then show some Eskimo art of the same animals. Ask students what liberties the artists have taken with their subjects. How have they exaggerated certain features? Point out that some primitive art is similar to modern art; in both types of art, artists alter reality for the sake of artistic expression. A look at some 20th century sculpture of animals would illustrate this point.

READING SKILLS

Objective vs. Subjective: Ask students to make a statement of the basic argument presented in this article. (Example: Are outside influences a good or a bad thing for the art of a primitive culture?) Then ask students to reread the article and search for clues to the author's point of view. (There aren't any.) Point out that it is impossible to tell on which side of this issue the author's sympathy lies.

Conclusion: Have students reread the last paragraph. Does it sum up the article for us? No. Point out that newspaper articles often conclude with less important information. The reason? The journalist knows that, when the newspaper layout is made, space considerations may require the deletion of the last several paragraphs. Ask students to consider this: how many paragraphs could have been cut from the end of this article before losing the main arguments on each side of the issue?

WORD STUDY

Word Parts and Word Origins: Have students use a desk-size or unabridged English dictionary (not a paperback or bilingual dictionary) to search for the meanings of word parts and the word origins of these words from the text:

- *animistic* (paragraph l) : *anima* comes from Latin. It means life principle, soul, air or breath. Discuss the meanings of *animism, an animated person* and *an animated film.*
- *sophisticated* (paragraph 3): Have students check the origins of words beginning with *soph.* Discuss the meanings of *sophisticated, sophism* and *sophomore.*
- *aboriginals* (paragraph 3) : *Ab* means "from" and *origo* means "origin." *Aboriginals* refers to the first or original inhabitants of a country (the native or indigenous peoples). Have students compare this word to *origin* and *original.*

Word Meanings: Discuss ways that these two words are used:

- *dilute* (paragraph 4): Is there a relationship between this use of *dilute* and diluting a beverage?
- *purists* (paragraph 4, 11) : Ask students to define the word based upon its use in these paragraphs. Does the word have negative connotations? (Yes.) Could it be used to talk about other fields besides art? (Yes.)

EXTENDED ACTIVITIES

Viewing Eskimo Life: Show the class a short film or videotape about Eskimo life.

Seeing Eskimo Art: Visit an art museum or gallery that has an exhibit of Eskimo art.

Debate: Have a classroom discussion or debate involving these questions: Does ethnic art deteriorate in quality when (1) it becomes "impure" because the artists come in contact with other cultures and learn to use new mediums and techniques? (2) artists receive input from prospective buyers before their work is finished? (3) there is mass production of some works because they sell well?

Business: Article 3

Anxiously, Some Everyday Russians Are Making Their Own Mark on the Economy

BACKGROUND

After the Russian revolution in 1917, people living in what was the Soviet Union were secure in their jobs. They were told where to work, what to do and how to do it. Businesses were owned by the government, and bureaucrats decided what to make and how much to sell the products for. Workers were guaranteed employment, although they might have limited opportunity to advance in their careers.

All of that changed in 1991 when the communist system collapsed in eastern Europe. The economy of eastern Europe is now being transformed into a market economy, and businesses are being turned over to private companies. Decisions as to what to manufacture, how much to sell products for and how much to pay employees are now being made on the basis of demand. Products that can be sold most profitably are now more likely to be produced. Wages are more closely related to the value of workers' skills. In addition, prices, no longer controlled by the government, have risen sharply. Many workers have been caught in a squeeze. Unemployment, which was unknown in the communist era, has been growing. So, many Russians, like the Zverevs and Stepanovs in the article, have had to find new and creative ways to earn a living or supplement their salaries. As a result, today's Russians are gradually turning into the entrepreneurs that their government once described as the enemy.

Explanation of Terms:
The battered *Zhiguli* that the Zverevs are all washing is a car that was designed in Italy by Fiat Motors and then produced in Russia, where it became quite popular.

Definitions of Some Business Terms in the Article:

Goods are things one can buy, such as groceries, clothing and furniture.

Services are acts that someone does for a customer or client, such as cutting hair or providing legal advice.

Barter means trading goods or services for other goods or services. In the article, Stepanov barters his eggs and veal to get goods and services in return.

Market economy means that prices and wages are determined by the cost of producing a product and the rate of demand for it. Goods and services must be sold for enough money to pay for the cost of production and to provide a profit for the manufacturer. Otherwise, the company that makes the product will lose money and, eventually, go out of business.

Solvent, in an economic sense, means getting enough income to meet expenses.

Vouchers are paper credits given to people to use instead of money to purchase goods or services. The article refers to lunch vouchers. These are used by the workers to purchase lunch at the cafeteria.

Shares are units of ownership in a business. Companies usually sell shares (of stock) to the public. Each share represents a part ownership in the company. Shares entitle the owner to choose who will run the business and, if the company is profitable, to share in the profits.

A *dividend* is money paid to shareholders as their part of the profits.

RELATED READINGS

Articles in the Text: The second article in the Education section—"Moscow Chefs: Where's the Beef?"—is also about ingenious ways of dealing with problems of the Russian economy.

AUDIOVISUAL AIDS

- The article is recorded on the audiocassettes accompanying the program.

READING SKILLS

Comparison and Contrast: Have students reread paragraphs 11 to 16, and then make a chart listing the differences between Cafeteria No. 20 under the old system (government-owned and operated) and the new, privatized system.

Making Inferences: In paragraph l, the author speaks of "Russia's bet on the West." Ask students what he is implying? Is he sure that capitalism will work there, will bring prosperity? In paragraph 4, when the author says "the family . . . was approached," who probably approached them?

WORD STUDY

Expression *As Well:* Point out *as well* in paragraph 2, and ask students to define it. (It means *also.*)

Business Vocabulary: Discuss the meanings of the following words commonly used in the business world: *bargain* (paragraph 9), *shortage* (paragraph 19), *discount* (paragraph 22), *cooperative* (paragraph 30). Also compare the meaning of *share* (paragraph 12) when speaking of stock in a company and *share* in its more general meaning.

Analyzing Phrases: In paragraph 19, students will find the phrases *on short notice* and *in short supply.* Ask the class: In which expression does short refer to time? in which to the amount of something? (*Short notice* means with very little time between when something is requested and when it is supposed to be done. *Short supply* means a small, inadequate amount.)

Pronunciation: Have students pronounce these words from the article, and then discuss their meanings: *entrepreneurship* (paragraph 2), *regime* (paragraph 9) and *debts* (paragraph 29) *Entrepreneur* comes from the French word meaning "to undertake." The suffix *-ship* is a noun ending that means the quality or condition of something. *Regime* means a political or social system and contains the sound [zh], which is also in the words *television, measure* and *garage.* Point out that, in the word *debt*, the *b* is silent.

GRAMMAR AND SENTENCE PATTERNS

Collective Nouns: Family is a good example of a collective noun. Point out that a collective noun usually takes a singular verb. (See paragraph 1: "the Zverev family is" and paragraph 4: "the family . . . was approached.") But also notice that in paragraph 1, the pronoun *they* is used to refer to the family. Why? To use *it* would be confusing since the family members are people, not things. When a sentence speaks of the members of a group acting individually, then a plural verb or a plural pronoun may be used. To give students practice with collective nouns, play a game. Form teams of two or three and see which team can list the most collective nouns in three minutes. (Some common examples are class, group, team, orchestra, band, committee, club and faculty.)

STYLE AND TONE

Figurative Language: Discuss the figurative comparison used in paragraph 3, sentence 1. In comparing Soviet habits to "thick sludge," does the author suggest that these habits are easy or difficult to change?

EXTENDED ACTIVITIES

Getting Up-to-Date Information: Have students look for magazine and/or newspaper articles about Russia and some of the other former Soviet Union republics. Is the economy better, worse or about the same as it was in 1992?

Business: Article 4

King of the Court: High-Tech, High-Price Sneakers

BACKGROUND

Athletic shoes were once reserved for use in the gym. But with two trends that began in the late seventies, the cult of physical fitness and the growth of the designer clothing market, athletic shoes are seen ever more frequently on the most fashionable urban and suburban streets. Why this desire to dress, at least from the ankle down, like a "jock" (a person involved in athletics)? Jocks are young and physically fit. As the U.S. population ages, baby boomers—the postwar generation born between 1945 and 1956—want to think of themselves as youthful. They may tell you that they wear the shoes for comfort, but there is obviously more involved. More and more career women wear their Nikes and Reeboks to "power walk" (show that they have important jobs) to work, where they change into classic-style high heels. As middle-aged men begin to buy "relaxed" (roomier in the waist and hips) blue jeans, they continue to lace up their high-priced youth-oriented footwear.

In addition to the desire to retain a youthful identity and appear athletic, people gain another status symbol by purchasing these shoes. Their designer labels, like those of many clothes marketed, are on the outside of the item. One's peers need be able only to recognize the logo on a piece of clothing to know that money has been invested to make a fashion statement. Many items of everyday wear—shirts, blouses, sweat pants, purses and gym bags—boldly display the name of the designer. This display turns consumers into walking advertisements. Still, designer clothes are the dress of choice for many.

Another factor leading to the mass popularity of athletic shoes is the worship of the athletes who sell them. Popular role models like the basketball superstar Michael Jordan become fashion plates, each with his or her own set of products. Finally, in an age when advancements in technology constantly occur, it is also significant that these shoes make scientific claims for design. While traditionalists may choose Converse All-Stars in a rainbow of colors, technology-minded consumers opt for bladders, pumps and new materials. The "technology" put into the shoes is designed to give a competitive edge to the manufacturer, and not just to the athlete.

RELATED READINGS

Articles in the Text: Several other articles treat marketing: "New Under the Tree: Computers for Tots" (Education section) and "EC Sets 'Ecolabel' for Green Products" (News section). They might be discussed along with this article. All three deal with creating a wider market for an existing product or relabeling products to appeal in a new way.

Items in the News: Have students locate other articles about marketing strategies for discussion in class. They might want to focus on the issue of celebrity endorsements in particular.

AUDIOVISUAL AIDS

- Bring to class some glossy magazine ads containing athletes' endorsements of products, athletic shoes if possible.
- Bring an actual pair of high-style, high-tech athletic shoes to class to show the students if they are unfamiliar with the item.

  If several members of the class already own such shoes, however, have them compare and contrast the different brands.
- The article is recorded on the audiocassettes accompanying the program.

READING SKILLS

Making Inferences: The psychology of marketing demands that products fulfill a need for consumers. Did a need exist for the athletic shoes described in the article? How was it created? What information does the article provide on the subject? What is the opinion of students beyond what is presented in the article?

Categorizing: This article was placed in the Business section and not the Sports section. Have students decide in which section they think it fits better and list reasons to defend their choice.

WORD STUDY

Meanings: Discuss the meaning of the following words in the article related to marketing and sales: *niche, wholesale, brands* (paragraph 4); *market saturation* (paragraph 5); *spokesman* (paragraph 8); *retailers* (paragraph 14); *promotion* (paragraph 15); *revenue* (paragraph 25); *hype* (paragraph 28). Have students use a dictionary if necessary.

Adjectives: Point out the number of hyphenated adjective phrases in the article: *high-tech, high-price* (headline); *low-tech, black-and-white, light-weight, high-contrast* (paragraph 2); *play-related* (paragraph 14); *high-visibility* (paragraph 23). Have students indicate the noun that each adjective describes.

GRAMMAR AND SENTENCE PATTERNS

Sentence Connectors: The words *but* and *and* are commonly used to connect two sentences. When they connect sentences, they are usually preceded by a comma. In this article, however, and in informal English in general, they are used to begin new sentences. Note the first sentences of paragraphs 3, 6 and 9.

More formal words or phrases such as *in addition, additionally,* and *furthermore* can be substituted for *and.* Similarly, words and phrases including *however, on the contrary* and *in contrast* can replace *but.* Have students write sets of sentences using these connecting words.

NUMBERS AND MEASUREMENTS

Students may want to make a list of the frequent use of percentages in this article. What are they used to compare? (See paragraphs 4, 5, 9, 12 and 14.)

EXTENDED ACTIVITIES

Survey: Have students survey wearers of best-selling athletic shoes for the reasons they purchased them. Use paragraph 14 as a guide for questions.

SECTION 4: EDUCATION

Education: Article 1

New Under the Tree: Computers for Tots

BACKGROUND

Computers are now a common sight in elementary schools in the United States, where they are used for the study of math, science, reading, geography and writing. If the makers of computers have their way, they may soon be standard equipment in preschools as well. The industry has discovered a new market for their high-tech invention, the 2-year-old to 5-year-old set. Computers are being adopted with enthusiasm by ambitious parents, who want the best in life for their children. Computer makers are aware of the educational trend toward reading and math readiness, which suggests to parents that preschoolers master basic skills before formal schooling begins. Computers for tots, as the article states, are refined video games designed to stress readiness skills. Instead of shooting down flying saucers or finding hidden treasures as video arcade games often do, the preschool computers teach shapes, numbers, letters and the names of common objects.

But critics claim that the computers may be unnecessary for young children, who can learn these elementary skills through traditional play with colorful blocks, puzzles and cutouts of alphabet letters and numbers. Moreover, they claim that part of early learning involves human contact for rewards and human interaction for socialization, neither of which can be taught by computers. Still, advocates of early childhood computers cite the "user-friendly" quality of their inventions, which cheer, sing, talk or flash bright lights when a child answers successfully. In addition, they claim that the early introduction of computers is just another readiness skill necessary for the students of tomorrow.

As both sides argue, companies making computers increase their sales. It is estimated that by the year 2000 computers will be the second-largest industry in the world in terms of revenue. Today the number of computers worldwide stands at over 100 million and is growing daily. From a mere dozen companies in the early 1960s, the industry has grown to more than 10,000 firms worldwide. These companies manufacture computers, software and peripheral equipment such as modems and printers. In the United States, the largest computer company is IBM (International Business Machine Corporation). In the late 1980s, IBM's sales topped $50 billion. Outside of the United States, the largest computer manufacturer is Fujitsu, whose sales topped $9 billion in 1988. European computer leaders include Groupe Bull of France, Olivetti of Italy and Siemens AG of Germany.

Many computer companies as well as toy makers have entered the preschool market with a variety of innovative computers, which include talking toy robots, teddy bears and life-size dolls programmed to teach foreign languages. These items are commanding more and more shelf space at large toy and department stores. Although most of these toys are simply programmed, they represent great advances in their ability to respond in a "human" manner to the child. Although computers cannot replace parents or teachers as primary sources of knowledge, they are an early way of learning for more and more children worldwide. "Turn on the computer, Mommy" is now as familiar a request as "Will you read me a story, Daddy?" in many homes.

RELATED READINGS

Articles in the Text: "Man Still Beats Chess Machine, for Now" (Sports section) focuses on another use of the computer—this time in a way that aims at imitating human intelligence. That article might be compared with this article for a discussion of the value of the new computer applications. Two other articles in the Education section, "What's in a Gesture? Kids Need to Learn" and "For Japanese, Cramming for Exams Starts Where the Cradle Leaves Off," deal with childhood education and might be discussed along with this article.

Items in the News: The Business section and Arts and Leisure section of newspapers often contain regular columns on computers. Have students watch for any stories that pertain to the use of computers for education to bring to class for discussion.

AUDIOVISUAL AIDS

- If possible, bring a preschool computer to class. Have the students work with it and evaluate its usefulness for children.
- Bring a catalog containing computers and/or software programs for children to class. Show the pictures and read the descriptions with the students. Have students judge the usefulness of the products advertised.
- The article is recorded on the audiocassettes accompanying the program.

READING SKILLS

Using Examples: Have students categorize the types of examples used in the article. For instance, the first six paragraphs make up an introductory anecdote. Have them find another anecdote (paragraphs 23-25), various descriptions (paragraphs 10, 11, 15, 20 and 21), and direct quotations (paragraphs 12, 13, 14, 27 and 28).

Categorizing: This article was placed in the Education section and not the Business section. Have students decide in which section they think it fits better and list reasons to defend their choice.

WORD STUDY

Imitative Words: Words that sound like the action or event they describe are called imitative words. Another name for such "sound" words is "onomatopoeia," which is from the Greek, meaning "coining of words." Words such as *buzz, crack* and *cuckoo* are examples of imitative words. Ask students what these sound words imitate. Then call their attention to the imitative word *blip* (paragraph 8), a word originally meaning a spot of light on a radar screen accompanied by a sound. Two other imitative words are *beep* and *click* (paragraph 2). Ask students to think of more words like these in English or in another language they know.

Prefixes: The prefix *pre-* means "before." Note its use in preschool. Preschool children refer to children under the age of five or six when they begin formal schooling in the U.S.

Parts of Speech: Have students look at the various word forms related to *prepare* (v.) : *preparation* (n.), *preparedness* (n.), *prepared* (adj.) and *preparatory* (adj.). Have them explain the difference between the two nouns and the two adjectives, using a dictionary.

GRAMMAR AND SENTENCE PATTERNS

Imperatives: Notice in paragraph 10 that the sentences are imperatives or command sentences. Imperatives always imply the second person subject, you. Have students write a series of instructions on the use of some object in the classroom (e.g., overhead projector, video machine) or some other machine that they use commonly. Have them begin each step with an imperative.

EXTENDED ACTIVITIES

Store Visit: Take a class trip to a department store that has a good supply of early childhood computers. Have students decide which computers to purchase. In class, discuss why they chose the particular computers.

Class Visit: Have students observe a preschool class at play. Have them take notes on the activities that engage the children. What activities would be enhanced by computers? In what activities are computers irrelevant?

Education: Article 2

Moscow Chefs: Where's the Beef?

BACKGROUND

Founded in 1147, Moscow is a city of 8.5 million people. The capital and largest city of the former Soviet Union and of Russia, it is the fourth-largest city in the world and ranks first in Europe. Once the home of the czars, Moscow is filled with palaces, museums and art treasures.

Travelers to the city, through which the Moscow River flows, will find the city laid out in the shape of a wheel, with wide spokelike streets that cross circular boulevards. The Kremlin stands at the center of this wheel.

Inside the walls of the Kremlin are ornate cathedrals, palaces and government buildings. Some of the cathedrals were built in the 1400s, and many of the czars are buried in the Cathedral of the Archangel Michael.

In addition to the stately government buildings and cathedrals, Moscow boasts the famous Moscow State University (established in 1755), one of the world's largest libraries and the Bolshoi Theater, where world-renowned Russian ballets are interpreted by internationally acclaimed dancers. For further amusement, Muscovites go to Gorky Park, a popular amusement center with boating, ice skating and tennis, or to Luzhniki, a 103,000-seat sports stadium mainly used for soccer.

Because matters of cuisine were deemphasized under the Soviet regime as decadent pleasures and because of food shortages that plague the republic of Russia, tourists do not travel to Moscow in search of good food. And the very idea of a Russian cooking school may strike readers accustomed to the tradition of fine cuisine established in such countries as France and Italy as rather absurd. But there is, in fact, a cuisine native to Russia, which includes some of the world's best caviar, smoked fish, tasty dumplings, breads and borscht (a soup made with beets or spinach).

Despite these interesting native delicacies, the problem for the students at Professional Technical School No. 41 is twofold. First, they must cope with the shortages that this article so aptly describes. Second, they must adapt to the new openness of the Russian economy as Western chefs establish joint-venture restaurants and large American corporations like Pizza Hut and MacDonalds open brightly lit eateries on Moscow's ancient streets.

The reader of this article must cope with a kind of technical vocabulary: French words used in cooking—from the word *cuisine* itself, to the words *chef, repertoire* and *torte.* Of course, these are just a few of the words that make up the French lexicon of cooking. Verbs for cooking such as *sauté* and *flambé,* and nouns like *soufflé, bouillabaisse, paté,* and *terrine* are also derived from the French. Just hearing them might make the reader of this article hungry!

RELATED READINGS

Articles in the Text: Several other articles deal with food or eating habits: "Hold Your Nose at the Steak House" in the Opinion section discusses the beef industry, and "Food for Luck" in the Arts and Leisure section provides an international perspective on odd food habits. For more information on Russia, students can read "Anxiously, Some Russians Are Making Their Own Mark on the Economy" in the Business section.

Items in the News: Have students clip articles that discuss economic and cultural developments in Russia for discussion in class. Students might also clip articles from newspaper food sections for a discussion of international recipes.

AUDIOVISUAL AIDS

- Bring photos to class of typically Russian foods such as caviar, lox and borscht.
- Bring cookbooks to class containing a variety of international recipes, including those from Russia.
- The article is recorded on the audiocassettes accompanying the program.

READING SKILLS

Cause and Effect: Paragraph 7 states that "for the last 70 years[,] food has been viewed more as fuel for human workers than something to be savored and enjoyed." Discuss this as a cause for some of the problems at Professional Technical School No. 41.

Gathering Details: The article gives many details that let the reader know a great deal about the cooking school and its methods. Have students describe the school in as much detail as possible, using the information supplied in the article.

WORD STUDY

Synonyms: Examine the related words in the article, all of which are the opposite of *real: fake* (paragraph 3), *synthetic* (paragraph 3), *wax model* (paragraph 4). Are some more positive than others? Other negative words that also mean fake are *phoney* and *fraudulent.* Ask students if these words could be used at any point in the article.

Suffixes: The suffix *-less* means "without." Examine its use in *bloodless* (paragraph 6). Extend its use by introducing the word *meatless.* Have students think of other English words using this suffix (hairless, lifeless, hopeless).

Food Vocabulary: Because of the many food words, review food vocabulary with students. One approach would be to have students find and classify all the food vocabulary in the article (e.g., meat, vegetables, cakes, methods of cooking). Then have students add as many words as possible to each category.

STYLE AND TONE

Descriptive Words: Point out the many descriptive verbs used to help readers get the "flavor" of a Russian cooking class. The description begins with paragraph 15: *clustered* (paragraph 15), *smirked and snickered* (paragraph 17), *hissed and skulked* (paragraph 19). Have students use a dictionary to get the connotations of each of the verbs.

NUMBERS AND MEASUREMENTS

Though measurements for particular recipes are not given within this article, have students bring in a recipe using grams and liters and convert the measures to ounces, pints and so on.

EXTENDED ACTIVITIES

Cooking Demonstration: If facilities permit, turn the class into a cooking school by having students volunteer to make dishes in the classroom.

Recipe Exchange: Have students share some of their favorite recipes with their classmates.

Russian Cuisine: Bring Russian cuisine items to class for students to share, or, if possible, go on a class trip to a Russian restaurant, bakery or delicatessen.

Education: Article 3

For Japanese, Cramming for Exams Starts Where the Cradle Leaves Off

BACKGROUND

Though this article is critical of the intense, all-consuming nature of the Japanese educational system, one must give credit where credit is due. Because it has a highly educated population, Japan has been able to accomplish quite a lot. Today, it is one of the world leaders in trade and industry. Nearly all its people are literate. Medical care is excellent, and life expectancy is among the highest in the world. The Japanese enjoy many benefits that come from having a highly educated population.

What sort of formal education do private jukus supplement? In Japan, public education is free and compulsory for all children between the ages of 6 and 15. This includes six years of elementary school and three years of junior high school. Students attend school 5 1/2 days a week. The school year goes from April through to the following March.

Theoretically, Japanese students have a vacation from late July through August. However, during that time, many attend jukus to prepare for those all-important national exams that decide their fate. Tests given before junior high school determine who goes to the better schools. Then, in order to be admitted to senior high school, students must pass another exam three years later. More than 90 percent of all students (female as well as male) go on to high school. About one third of Japanese students then go on to some form of higher education, either a university, college or trade school.

Because admission to the better schools is highly competitive, students spend many hours attending jukus and doing homework for their jukus in order to prepare for "examination hell." Why is it so important to get into a prestigious university? Students who get accepted to the best universities are likely to be professionally set for life. After graduation, major corporations and government ministries will offer them jobs. The two-day tests that these 18-year-olds take can make or break their entire careers.

Thus, one can see the dilemma of Japanese parents. They may not want to see their children studying 12 hours a day. But they know that success in an adult career depends upon getting into the right academic track early in life. For this reason, Japanese mothers become "education Mamas." They are considered responsible for their children's academic success or failure. Therefore, they often consult with their children's teachers, visit the classroom and tutor their youngsters at home.

Many juku teachers advise students to study 10 hours a day, and some very ambitious students exceed that. Why, one wonders, should Japanese children need to study so much? For one thing, their written language is the most complex and most difficult of all the writing systems in the world. Along with Japanese phonetic symbols, the language uses Chinese characters, each of which stands for a complete word or syllable. Minimal literacy requires mastery of at least 1,850 characters. In addition to all this, Japanese students must learn the Latin alphabet and three systems of romanized Japanese. Of course, many Japanese students also study English.

With all this studying, how can there be enough time for students to enjoy life and develop their nonacademic talents and interests? Also, is all this academic pressure too much psychological stress for young people? These are some of the issues this article raises.

RELATED READINGS

Articles in the Text: The virtue of hard work is taught to Japanese from early childhood on. As a result, Japan is now trying to deal with an adult malady called *karoshi,* which means death from overwork. For more information about the need for more leisure in the life of the Japanese, read "Hey Give Yourself a Break and Go Jump in a Hole" (in the Arts and Leisure section of the text) and look at the background notes for that article in this Instructor's Manual. American parents, too, sometimes "push" their children too hard. Students can compare this article about the Japanese with the first article in the Education section.

AUDIOVISUAL AIDS

Use a map to introduce some important geographical facts about Japan. Japan is an island nation. Its territory consists of four main islands and groups of smaller ones that extend in a series of arcs for about 3,000 kilometers (1,875 miles). Much of the land is mountainous. Almost the entire population of 124 million lives on just 16 percent of the land, the part that is level enough for settlement and development. Most Japanese live near the coasts in urban areas. The population density of these areas is the highest in the world. Japan, with less land than France, has about double the population. Could overcrowding have any connection with the competitive nature of the Japanese? It is an interesting question to discuss.

READING SKILLS

Making Inferences: Paragraph 7 says that jukus are praised as "a reflection of a system of advancement based on merit alone." Ask students to note that quotation and then look in paragraph 9 for evidence that contradicts it. (Obviously, wealthier parents can afford to send their children to more and better jukus.)

Comparisons: Have students list all the arguments for and against the jukus, as given in the article, listing paragraph numbers.

WORD STUDY

Phonics and Pronunciation: Review the phonics rules regarding "hard" and "soft" *c* and *g* by using words from the article. (The "soft" sounds usually precede the letters *e, i* and *y*.) Write these words on the board, and have students pronounce them:

Words with *c:* circle, succeed, success, criticize, reducing, curriculum, secret, competition

Words with *g:* advantage, prestigious, goal, generation, dragon, gain, eager

Note: With *g*, there are many exceptions to the rule. One exception from the article is *eager*. Some other common exceptions are *girl, give, gift and get.*

STYLE AND TONE

Connotations: The author of this article translates juku as cram school, a term loaded with negative overtones. A more neutral translation that is sometimes used is after-hour school. In paragraph 18, the author does not say that exams are given to the students (neutral language). Instead, he writes of "examination hell" inflicted on children. Also, calling them children instead of students makes the whole ordeal of these standardized national tests sound even worse. Point this word choice out to students.

EXTENDED ACTIVITIES

Guest Speaker: Invite someone who has been educated in Japan to talk to the class. Before the visit, have students work in groups to prepare questions for the visitor.

Discussion: Have students discuss the qualities of a good education, covering such factors as the role of competitive examinations, alternate schools such as jukus, and the role of nonacademic activities.

Education: Article 4

What's in a Gesture? Kids Need to Know

BACKGROUND

Nonverbal messages are sent in many ways, including facial expression, position and movement of the body, tone of voice, clothing, odor, touch and use of space. This area of study goes back at least as far as the 1800s, when teachers of acting analyzed the ways in which facial expressions and motions of the body could help an actor convey emotion. But as an area of scientific study, nonverbal communication is a twentieth century phenomenon.

Nonverbal communication is sometimes called body language. In academic circles, it encompasses two main areas of investigation. One is *kinesics,* the study of body and facial movements as they accompany speech. The other is *proxemics,* the study of ways in which people in different cultures use nonverbal means to convey feelings and social status. Ray L. Birdwhisstell and Edward T. Hall, both American anthropologists, developed these two sciences respectively.

In his popular book *Body Language,* Julius Fast says that nonverbal language is partly instinctive, partly learned and partly imitated. The meaning of a smile or a frown seems to be universal. But the meaning of a headshake varies from one culture to another. Westerners shake their heads up and down to say yes and sideways to say no. In some societies in India, the signals are reversed. When one person stands very close to another, it may indicate a desire for intimacy, or it may express aggressive, threatening feelings. However, in some cultures, standing very close is the norm.

The eyes are important nonverbal communicators. An increase in the size of the pupils is an indication of growing interest in or excitement about the person or thing being observed. Direct eye contact between social unequals is polite in some cultures and disrespectful in others.

Many people are interested in nonverbal communication because they believe it can help them. First, they hope to be able to adjust their nonverbal behavior to make a more favorable impression. Second, they hope to be able to "read" the signals sent by others, to understand and evaluate other people better. These are worthy goals, but they are not so easy to accomplish. Edward T. Hall, the founder of proxemics, writing in *Beyond Culture,* points out, "The language of behavior is extraordinarily subtle." Furthermore, "nonverbal systems are closely tied to ethnicity." Hall writes about Americans overseas who had to "adjust their behavior to people who kept them waiting, came an hour early to dinner (out of respect), or stood too close."

A recent *International Herald Tribune* (August 20, 1992) article provided more information about Dr. Stephen Nowicki and Dr. Marshall P. Duke's work with children who have social problems because of what these psychologists call *dyssemia.* The name comes from Greek word parts. *Dys-* means difficult; *semeia* means signals. In their new book *Helping the Child Who Doesn't Fit In,* Drs. Nowicki and Duke give some interesting statistics: in face-to-face interactions, only 7 percent of emotional meaning is expressed with words; 55 percent is expressed through facial expressions and 38 percent through tone of voice. The psychologists have also discovered that about 10 percent of children have one or more problems in transmitting or receiving nonverbal signals. By showing children what they are doing and how their behavior looks to others, these researchers are able to help them.

RELATED READINGS

Additional Readings: Axtell, Roger E. *Gestures: The Do's and Taboos of Body Language Around the World.* New York: John Wiley & Sons, Inc., 1991.

Fast, Julius. *Body Language.* New York: Simon and Schuster, 1970.

Hall, Edward T. *The Silent Language.* Garden City, NY: Doubleday, 1959.

Hall, Edward T. *Beyond Culture.* Garden City, NY: Doubleday, 1976.

Nowicki, Stephen, Jr., and Duke, Marshall P. *Helping the Child Who Doesn't Fit In.* Atlanta, GA: Peachtree Publishers, 1992.

READING SKILLS

Use of the Colon: Point out that a colon is often used to relate two ideas. Then have students find the colon in paragraph 2, and discuss its use (it introduces a set of examples).

Scanning: Have students practice scanning the article to look for (1) two phrases that mean *for example.* (The answers are *for instance,* in paragraphs 2 and 3 and *such as* in paragraph 17.) (2) two examples of tests that require an active response.

WORD STUDY

The Word *Hypothetical:* Discuss the meaning of the word, and note its use in paragraph 5. What is the usual reason that a speaker or writer talks about a hypothetical situation? What is a scientific hypothesis?

Negative Prefixes: Continue the study of negative prefixes introduced in the student text exercises. Point out that there are many negative prefixes in English, the most common of which are *in-, im-, un-, non-, dis-, il-* and *ir-*. Words beginning with *l* take the *il* prefix, words beginning with *r* take the *ir* prefix and words beginning with *p* take the *im* prefix. Ask students to say these words aloud with the correct negative prefix.

1. logical
2. controlled
3. dependable
4. legal
5. possible
6. probable
7. regular
8. able
9. ability
10. interesting
11. important
12. consistent
13. successful
14. correct
15. religious

GRAMMAR AND SENTENCE PATTERNS

Adjective Clauses: Have students find the adjective clause, relative pronoun and pronoun reference in each of these sentences:

Paragraph 11, sentence one: (*that* refers to *overeagerness*)
Paragraph 12: (*that* refers to *frustration*)
Paragraph 14, last sentence: (*that* refers to *defeatism*)

EXTENDED ACTIVITIES

Analyzing Nonverbal Communication: Find an emotional scene in a videotaped movie or TV show. Show it in class without the sound, and ask students what they think the actors are saying and what emotions are being conveyed. Then replay the scene with the sound on. Using another emotional scene, press pause and have students analyze the still picture. What facial expressions and gestures convey the various emotions?

SECTION 5: ARTS AND LEISURE

Arts and Leisure: Article 1

Food for Luck: New Year's Rituals

BACKGROUND

For thousands of years, people all over the world have celebrated the beginning of a new year. Despite differences in customs, new year's themes are remarkably similar throughout the world. These ideas seem to predominate: a need to review one's behavior during the past year; a desire to predict and perhaps also to influence the future; and a chance to start over, to wipe the slate clean and turn over a new leaf (as the expressions say). In some cultures, this last desire leads to customs such as doing a thorough housecleaning, making friends with an enemy, paying off debts or promising to improve in some way in the new year.

The Changing Dates of New Year's Day: When is New Year's Day? That depends upon what calendar the culture uses. Ancient civilizations recorded the passage of time in different ways: by phases of the moon (a lunar calendar), by the changing positional appearance of the sun in the sky (a solar calendar) or by a combination of both of these methods (a solar-lunar calendar). Ancient cultures celebrated the beginning of a new year on many different dates, most commonly at the beginning of a new season, especially fall or spring. (In fact, the word *year* comes from an old word meaning springtime.)

The old Roman calendar had only ten months, and New Year's Day was on March 1. Then, in 46 B.C., Julius Caesar introduced an improved calendar with twelve months and made New Year's Day on January 1. Caesar's calendar was designed with the advice of a Greek scientist named Sosigenes, who consulted experts in Egypt. The Egyptians had devised an excellent calendar based on the annual rise and fall of the Nile River. Their astronomers noted that a certain star, called Sirius, became visible just before the waters rose (about September 23). They measured their year from one appearance of this star to the next. That gave them a year with just over 365 days, the same as our present-day solar year. On Julius Caesar's calendar (called, in his honor, the Julian calendar) many of the months were named for Roman gods. January, for example, was named for Janus, the god who ruled over doors and gates. He had two faces, so he could see people entering and leaving. Similarly, at the beginning of a new year, we look both backward and forward.

The spread of Christianity resulted in a change in the Julian calendar. New Year's Day became a spring festival on March 25. However, in 1582, Pope Gregory XIII created the Gregorian calendar, and reinstated January 1 as the first day of the year. By 1600, many Western nations had adopted the Gregorian calendar. But England (and its American colonies) didn't make this change until 1752.

Today, the Gregorian calendar is used in most of the world, but some ethnic groups also observe other new year's celebrations. The Jewish people, for example, have a very serious new year—Rosh Hashanah—(head of the year) in the fall. The date is based upon the Jewish lunar calendar. The Chinese have a fifteen-day new year holiday, occurring in January or February. Its date is based upon the Chinese lunar calendar. Hindus in different parts of India celebrate the new year on various dates. Muslims use a calendar that has 354 days in most years, so, from year to year, the Muslim New Year falls on different dates on the Gregorian calendar.

Noise and Song: The custom of greeting the new year with loud noises goes back to ancient times. The purpose was to drive away evil spirits. Even today, in different countries, people bang on drums or pots, set off firecrackers, blow horns, ring bells and so on. In some parts of Scotland, young men and boys circle the houses of friends and relatives three times, shouting loudly. In Denmark, young people bang on their friends' doors.

An old Scottish song, with words written by Robert Burns more than 200 years ago, is also a new year's tradition in many countries. It honors old friends and past experiences.

Should auld acquaintance be forgot,
And never brought to mind?
Should auld acquaintance be forgot,
And days of auld lang syne?

Definitions of Foods Discussed in the Article:

chutney: an east Indian relish made with fruit and spices
collard greens: the leafy part of the collard, a type of kale
mulligatawny: an east Indian soup made with a meat base and seasoned with curry
truffles: rare, wild fungi that grow at the roots of oak and beech trees. The fruity body of the fungus is edible and used sparingly as a flavoring. Truffles are found by trained pigs or dogs that sniff out this expensive delicacy.
lasagna: an Italian dish made of wide pasta, meat and cheese
sauerkraut: a German dish made of thinly-shredded cabbage, cooked in brine. It can be served hot or cold.

RELATED READINGS

Additional Readings: Many children's books contain fascinating information about

New Year's customs from cultures around the world, written in a simple style quite accessible to ESL or EFL students. Here are a few titles:

Blackwood, Alan. *Holidays and Festivals: New Year.* Vero Beach, FL: Rourke Enterprises, 1987.

Brown, Tricia. *Chinese New Year.* New York: Henry Holt and Company, 1987.

Groh, Lynn. *A Holiday Book: New Year's Day.* Champaign, IL: Garrard Publishing Company, 1964.

AUDIOVISUAL AIDS

- If possible, show students a variety of calendars from different cultures.

READING SKILLS

Making Inferences: Ask students to make inferences about why people still practice customs described in the article, which, according to the author, are rooted in simplistic and primitive thought. Do people still believe in them, or is there another reason that they continue to practice them? Students should also be able to infer the reason for the 12 grapes mentioned in paragraph 6.

WORD STUDY

Word Meaning: In paragraph 7, why are the first hours of the new year called *delicate?* Ask students to think of some people and things that they sometimes describe as delicate.

Similar Words: Point out the differences in pronunciation and meaning between the word *recipes* (paragraph 1) and *receipt,* another word from the same Latin root. Also, discuss the differences between *rationale* (paragraph 13) and the word *rational.*

EXTENDED ACTIVITIES

Comparing Cultures: In a classroom where there is an ethnic mix, this article provides an excellent chance to share and compare traditions and beliefs. Here are some suggested activities:

1. Have students discuss (and perhaps bring samples) of traditional New Year's foods and customs in their culture. Students can teach each other how to say the traditional new year greeting in their language.
2. Working together, students can complete this chart:

Traditional Superstitions			
good luck	culture(s)	bad luck	culture(s)

Classroom Discussion: These questions should stimulate conversation.

1. Do you believe in good luck or bad luck?

2. Do you think that anything you do can influence your future? What? How?
3. If you could find out about your future, would you want to know?
4. What New Year's resolution (promise to improve) are you willing to make?

Arts and Leisure: Article 2

Hey, Give Yourself a Break and Go Jump in a Hole

BACKGROUND

"Take it easy," Americans often advise each other. "All work and no play makes Jack a dull boy." According to paragraph 4 of this article, pressure from other nations is forcing the Japanese government and big business to try to combat workaholism. But, in addition, the Japanese themselves recognize the need for change.

Since the late 1940s, Japanese workers have lived intimately with the all-too-common phenomenon of *karoshi* (death from overwork). Finally, in 1989, the syndrome received official recognition. Now, there are hundreds of health centers around the country fighting the condition. In addition, there's a telephone hotline to serve those at risk. Exactly what is *karoshi?* It's a fatal syndrome (group of symptoms that occur together) including apoplexy and high blood pressure. The cause: too many hours on the job.

After cancer, *karoshi* is now the second-leading cause of death among Japanese workers, claiming about 30,000 victims annually. According to the director of one *karoshi* clinic, "Japan's economic prosperity has taken a terrible toll on its people."

What can be done to help overworked Japanese employees? Two obvious answers are fewer hours at work and more hours on vacation. According to this article, Japanese employees work about 200 hours a year more than their American counterparts (see paragraph 5). Some victims of *karoshi* have been known to work 15-hour days on a regular basis.

In the U.S., most workers receive at least a two-week paid summer vacation plus many other days off for holidays and "sick days." In Japan in 1992, the average summer holiday was 7.4 days and even less for those employed by smaller companies.

Long workdays and short summer holidays have been the norm in Japan since the post-World War II period, when the country felt a great drive to rebuild as rapidly as possible. Moreover, Japanese culture glorifies work and frowns upon idleness.

But today the Japanese government is promoting leisure. Vacationing far from home is expensive and also exhausting because traffic on Japanese roads is terrible during summer holiday periods. So the idea of having more recreational facilities in the highly populated areas seems the perfect solution. Since the end of World War II, Japan has been inundated with Western (especially American) popular culture. The opening of a 204-acre Disneyland near Tokyo in 1983 was a major contribution to this trend. This article also mentions Sesame Land, a theme park named after a popular American TV show for children. Its main characters are talking puppets named Bert, Ernie and Oscar (a very grouchy green monster, who lives in a garbage can).

The recreational facilities discussed in this article may be just what the *karoshi* doctor ordered—so long as Japanese workers don't approach recreation with the same drive and push for endurance that they bring to their jobs. After all, relaxing and having fun are not so much determined by the activity as by the participant's attitude toward it. Consider, for example, the author of this article. Tokyo sky diving probably didn't do his health any good.

RELATED READINGS

Articles in the Text: The text contains two other articles about Japan. In the Education section, there's "For Japanese, Cramming for Exams Starts Where the Cradle Leaves Off," which is about overworked Japanese students. It echoes many of the ideas in this reading. In the Business section, there is "Sociology of the Kimono: Everything Young Is Old."

AUDIOVISUAL AIDS

Show some photographs, a videotape or a short film about Japan to give students a sense of how crowded and built-up the cities are. (See also the notes for the Audiovisual Aids for the article "For Japanese, Cramming for Exams Starts Where the Cradle Leaves Off" in the Education section.)

- The article is recorded on the audiocassettes accompanying the program.

READING SKILLS

Scanning: Have students practice the skill of scanning an article for specific information by finding the paragraph that answers each of these questions and writing down its number.

1. Why is there a boom in leisure activities in Japan?
2. Why are the Japanese considered workaholics?
3. How have the Japanese dealt with the problem of having a shortage of space for outdoor recreation?
4. How can a person sky dive without a parachute?

Use of Quotation Marks: Quotation marks sometimes show a special use of a word: In paragraph 2, the author mentions *salarymen* (Japanese-employed businessmen) and *office ladies* (Japanese secretaries, often called OLs). He puts quotation marks around these words because they are not standard English terms, but rather reflect Japanese coining words out of English. Also, in paragraph 6, there are quotation marks around the word *leisure,* suggesting that this word was not being used in the usual way. Here the use is ironical: the author is questioning whether forced leisure is real leisure. Discuss these uses of quotation marks with students.

WORD STUDY

Word Meanings: In paragraph 4, the word *notion* is used, and in paragraph 19, the word *concept* is used. In general, both mean "idea." Ask students which word is more likely to be used to describe an important scientific idea. Which is a better word to describe a foolish or trivial idea?

Phrasal Verbs: In paragraph 8, the phrasal verb *make up for* appears. It means "compensate for." Have students think of meanings of *make up* and *make up with.* List them on the board.

Word Parts: In this reading four common word parts are used: *pre-*, *fore-*, *anthro-* and *-ologist.* Have students look up their meanings in a dictionary. Then see if the group can think of some words in which each word part is used.

GRAMMAR AND SENTENCE PATTERNS

Emphatic Past Tense: In paragraph 17, the statement beginning "It did seem like sky diving . . ." uses the emphatic past tense (did seem) instead of the simple past tense (seemed). Discuss the reasons for using this tense (to emphasize something surprising, to correct someone's mistake and so on). Have the class practice making sentences with the emphatic past tense and describing situations in which it would be appropriate.

STYLE AND TONE

Read paragraph 1 aloud in class, and point out the stylistic elements that make it entertaining and amusing, for example: (1) the rhyming of shaking and quaking; (2) the double meaning (both literal and figurative) of "plunging headlong" into the new craze; (3) the helmet that "seems much too thin" because the frightened author feels very vulnerable; (4) the concluding contradiction in terms: sky diving without a parachute.

EXTENDED ACTIVITIES

Defining Entertainment: Have students discuss the meanings of the words *leisure, recreation* and *entertainment* and give examples of each.

Differences in Leisure-Time Activities: Discuss how climate and geography affect choices of leisure-time activities in various countries.

Arts and Leisure: Article 3

Art, Photography, Copyright and the Law

BACKGROUND

The United States court system (at both the state and federal systems) usually has three levels. The lowest level is where cases are tried. It is usually called the circuit or district court. The second and third levels are where appeals are heard. The second level is called the appeals or appellate court. The highest level is the supreme court. In this article, the artist Jeff Koons was dissatisfied with the district court's decision that he was guilty of copyright infringement (using another person's artistic work without permission and/or payment). So he instructed his lawyer to take the case to the appeals court.

On April 2, 1992, the U.S. Court of Appeals in New York City denied Koons's attempt to overturn the district court decision. The Court of Appeals affirmed (agreed with) the decision of the lower court.

Koons's defeat was disturbing to some artists because they felt that the court's decision imposed limitations upon an artist's freedom of expression. Artists in the 20th century have often taken images from advertising and from popular products and used them in a work of art. One of the most famous examples is Andy Warhol's use of Campbell's soup cans, referred to in this article. Koons is not the first artist to be sued for using someone else's design. However, other cases involving this issue were settled out of court. The Koons case, therefore, established a legal precedent, and one of importance because the decision was confirmed by a federal appeals court.

Koons claimed that his sculpture "String of Puppies" was fair use because it was a parody and a form of social criticism. The appeals court panel of three judges did not agree. The judges said that Koons's sculpture did not criticize or comment upon Rogers's photograph; it merely copied the photograph. Another factor causing Koons to lose his case was that he had not used just a part of Rogers's photograph; he had used all of it. A third point was that in using this image without permission, Koons had adversely affected Rogers's chances for selling rights to it to other artists for other artistic uses.

Did the court judge Koons fairly? Some people defend Koons by pointing out that, in making its decision, the court looked at a photograph of Koons's work, compared it to Rogers's black-and-white photograph, and declared them "substantially similar. " But Koons's work was not a black-and-white photograph; it was a large, colorful wooden sculpture. Koons's lawyer argued that Koons had copied only factual information (which cannot be copyrighted) and not the expression of the facts. The court's response to this argument was that Koons had also copied the arrangement of the facts, which is a part of artistic expression.

The judges also noted this interesting sidelight on Koons's behavior: before sending the card to the Italian artisans who actually made the wooden sculptures, Koons tore off the back of the notecard on which Rogers's photograph appeared. That was where Rogers's credit and copyright symbol were displayed!

Students who follow the contemporary art scene may have heard of Koons and even seen some of his work. Many of his recent sculptures show explicitly sexual scenes.

Explanation of Terms:

The First Amendment: An amendment to the U.S. Constitution that guarantees freedom of speech and of the press, and thus freedom of expression in general. The first ten amendments, known as the Bill of Rights, became part of the U.S. Constitution in 1791, just a few years after the Constitution itself was adopted. These amendments were intended to protect individuals from government interference. Many consider them the very basis of individual liberty. So when artists appeal to the First Amendment, they are referring to their right of freedom of expression.

Pietà: A representation of the dead Jesus with his mother Mary, a subject common in Western art and the subject of a famous sculpture by the artist Michelangelo

Wall Street: The financial center of the United States, in New York City

RELATED READINGS

Additional Readings: Buskirk, Martha. "Appropriation Under the Gun." *Art in America,* June, 1992, pages 37+.

Plagens, Peter. "The Young and the Tasteless." *Newsweek,* November 1991, page 80.

"Art or Commerce?" *Vanity Fair,* November 1991, page 258.

AUDIOVISUAL AIDS

Students might enjoy viewing the works of other postmodern artists, especially Andy Warhol, mentioned in paragraph 26 of the article. Warhol also used images from popular culture in his works of art. In paragraph 25, the article refers to Marcel Duchamp, a famous twentieth century French artist. Some of his sculptures were called "ready-mades" or "found objects," because they were made with common items, such as a wine bottle rack.

After students compare and contrast (note similarities and differences) the works of Koons and Rogers, they might also give their opinions of the two images as art. Did the students like these works of art? Why, or why not?

READING SKILLS

Inference and Direct Statement: The idea that Jeff Koons is more interested in making money than in creating significant works of art is both implied and directly stated in this article. Have students look for examples of both types of statements. (Inferences can be found in paragraph 24. More direct statements can be found in paragraphs 23 and 28, once students understand the meaning of the word *market* in this context.)

Figurative and Literal Language: Have students discuss the two sentences in paragraph 3. Which statement mentions a figurative action? (Koons's supporters didn't literally applaud, but they approved of the high prices paid for his work.) What is the literal action that Rogers took in response?

WORD STUDY

Legal Vocabulary: The article contains many legal terms. Have students look up their meanings in a dictionary: *lawsuit* (5); *case, testified* (7); *ruled, charges* (8); *trial, damages* (9); *appealed* (10); *court order* (29).

Punctuation: In this article, the possessive forms of the artists' names are made by adding *'s* (Koons's and Rogers's). It is also correct to add just an apostrophe when making a singular word that ends in *s* possessive. (One could also write Koons' work or Rogers' work.)

Word Meanings: Discuss the meaning of the word *culture.* What do we mean when we describe a person as "cultured"? This article uses the word *culture* in two similar phrases: mass culture (paragraph 12) and popular culture (paragraph 13). Discuss what type of behavior, entertainment and so on is meant by these terms. What other types of culture are there?

Noun Endings: Have students pronounce these verb/noun pairs. Point out the two common noun endings: *tion* and *ment.*

infringe / infringement	deprive / deprivation
enforce / enforcement	intimidate / intimidation

Now have students use these words in a sentence. If they need help, ask questions, such as: Who or what infringes upon your freedom to do what you want? Who enforces the law? Who enforces the rules in school? Who intimidates you? Why? Have you ever been deprived of anything that you wanted? Why? Who deprived you of the thing you wanted?

GRAMMAR AND SENTENCE PATTERNS

Pronoun Reference: Have students find the antecedents for the following pronouns:

paragraph 5, sentence l, *which* (appeal)
paragraph 13, sentence 2, *he* (Koons)
paragraph 17, *it* (photograph)
paragraph 19, sentence l, *they* (Koons's lawyers)

EXTENDED ACTIVITIES

Public Speaking: Have students prepare a short speech about their favorite work of art. They should bring photographs (or the actual work) to show. The selections can range from a famous piece to a work of art the student owns. The speech should include the following information: the origin of the work (when and where it was made), the material(s) it was made of and the reason(s) the student likes it.

Group Trips: A class visit to an art gallery or an art museum would tie in well with this reading. If possible, see examples of postmodern art that use images from popular culture.

Arts and Leisure: Article 4

Is There a European Accent in Euro Disneyland?

BACKGROUND

Who was Walt Disney? Even before he opened huge theme parks, Disney was a famous American producer of animated cartoons, movies and TV shows. He was the creator of Donald Duck and Mickey Mouse (who is, according to studies, the world's most well-known face). Disney was a creative genius, as well as an American legend. His life is an outstanding example of two character traits that Americans admire greatly. Disney was a self-made man, growing up in a large, loving family that had no spare money to help him achieve his dreams. All that he accomplished was with his own skill and courage. Second,

Disney was an adventurer. He believed that life should be an exciting adventure, and he lived his own life that way, repeatedly risking his money and his reputation to try something new. Moreover, the films, TV shows and parks he built were designed to give others the excitement he loved. He once said of Disneyland, "It has that thing—that imagination and the feeling of happy excitement— I knew as a kid." One of his daughters once said, "My dad was a kid all his life." This childlike enthusiasm was one of his great gifts, and it inspired his creativity.

There is a long list of Walt Disney "firsts." His company created the first talking cartoon. It was Steamboat Willie, made in 1928 and starring Mickey Mouse. In 1932, Disney produced the first cartoons in color. In 1938, he created the first feature-length animated picture, *Snow White and the Seven Dwarfs.* In 1940, he used animation to interpret orchestral music visually in the great film classic *Fantasia.* In *Song of the South,* he combined live actors and cartoon characters in a full-length feature. In 1959, when TV was still young, he began producing TV shows. He also made conventional movies (with no cartoon characters) and wonderful documentaries about wildlife in natural surroundings.

"Walt never thought he was beaten at anything—ever," his wife Lillian once said. Here's an example of that spirit. In 1928, Disney's first successful cartoon character—Oswald the Lucky Rabbit—was stolen from him by a film distributor. After getting that bad news, on the train ride back home, Walt took out his sketch pad and created a new character—Mickey Mouse.

Disney was also a perfectionist. When filming the adventure movie *20,000 Leagues Under the Sea,* he was not satisfied with the squid attack scene. It wasn't exciting enough. "Add a storm," he said. Those three words cost the studio an additional $250,000, but the new scene was terrific. This desire to make things perfect to every detail is still characteristic of the Disney Company. It is reflected in the detail of the exhibits at the parks and in the neatness code mentioned in the first Euro Disney article.

Why did a filmmaker begin building theme parks? Disney explained it this way: "I happen to be a kind of inquisitive guy, and when I see things I don't like, I start thinking why do they have to be like this and how can I improve them." In the 1940s, Disney used to take his two daughters to amusement parks to go on the rides. The parks were dirty and in bad condition; the food they served was terrible. He started to think about how to improve them. The result: the Disney theme parks.

Disney Theme Parks Today and Tomorrow: Currently there are Disney parks in four locations near these large cities: Los Angeles, California; Orlando, Florida; Tokyo, Japan; and Paris, France. In addition to operating these parks and planning expansions, the Disney Company continues to make movies.

Euro Disney's Impact: The French feared that Euro Disney would "destroy the neighborhood." From the French perspective, the good news is that the park has not had a great negative impact upon its environment. Unlike the areas around the Disney parks in California and Florida, Euro Disney is not surrounded by inexpensive hotels, motels, restaurants and other businesses serving tourists. But there is some bad news, too.

Although Euro Disney has not yet swallowed up the area it resides in, it may do so in the future. Disney's plans call for a second theme park in 1995 and a third one by the year 2000. Moreover, these parks will be surrounded by one of the biggest real estate developments in Europe.

RELATED READINGS

Additional Readings: Students may enjoy reading a biography of Walt Disney. Much of the preceding information came from the following biography: Greene, Katherine and Richard. *The Man Behind the Magic.* New York: Viking Penguin, 1991. This text is written at a reading level that would be accessible to intermediate ESL students.

Items in the News: The Disney Company is involved in many different enterprises and is often written up in the daily newspaper. Encourage students to clip articles about Disney activities and share them with their classmates.

AUDIOVISUAL AIDS

If possible, the class should see at least a few Walt Disney cartoons with Mickey Mouse and Donald Duck. Also, parts of *Fantasia* would be ideal to show. (A new, improved version is available on videotape.) Students should also be encouraged to watch some of the full-length Disney films at home and share them with children.

- The main article is recorded on the audiocassettes accompanying the program.

READING SKILLS

Main Idea: Notice that the headline of the first article is a question. After reading the article carefully, students should be able to answer the question "yes" or "no" and give information from the article to support their answers.

Reading for Specific Information: Who owns the Walt Disney Company? Students should reread paragraphs 1, 5 and 9 in the follow-up article and then discuss the answer.

WORD STUDY

Word Meanings:

- Discuss the meaning of the word *icon,* used in paragraph 8 of the first article. Have students tell about other people or things that are considered icons.
- Paragraph 16 of the first article contains the clause "buccaneers in the pirate's lair will banter in French, Spanish and English." Have students use context clues to guess the meanings of the words *buccaneers, lair* and *banter.* Then have them check in a dictionary to see how close their guesses were.

STYLE AND TONE

Dialogue: Note that the first article begins with an imaginary conversation, although there are no quotation marks to signal a dialogue.

Figurative Language: The title of the follow-up article has both a literal and a figurative meaning. The gloss (or shine) is off because Euro Disney is not brand-new anymore. But, figuratively speaking, the glow of great expectations is also gone because the park hasn't done as well as expected.

EXTENDED ACTIVITIES

Visit to a Theme Park: If most of your students have never been to a theme park and there is one nearby, a class trip to the park would be excellent.

Studying Children's Stories: Have five groups read and prepare an oral report about one of these five stories: Sleeping Beauty, Cinderella, Pinocchio, Peter Pan and Alice in Wonderland. (All are mentioned in paragraphs 11 to 14 in the first article.) Students can then choose which group they wish to work on. Each group will read various versions of the designated story and participate in a panel that will tell the story to the rest of the class. Students can also comment on how the story varies from one culture to another and/or how it is used at a Disney theme park.

SECTION 6: SCIENCE AND ENVIRONMENT

Science and Environment: Article I

Even the Palawan Stink Badger Has Its Defenders

BACKGROUND

To understand this article, students must understand the meaning of the phrase *endangered species.* In this article, the word *species* refers to a biological category. Members of the same species are able to inbreed (have offspring together). An endangered species is one whose population has been so reduced in number that the group is threatened with extinction, or disappearing. Most biologists consider a species endangered if they expect it to disappear completely within 20 years, unless special efforts are made to protect it. At the present time, thousands of plants and animals are in this category.

During the millions of years that preceded the appearance of human life on earth, some plants and animals became extinct as the result of geologic and climatic changes that altered the environment. Today, environmental change remains the major threat to biological diversity. These kinds of changes occur very rapidly now due to human activity and modern technology.

One example is what is happening to tropical rain forests. As trees are cut down to develop an area for human habitation, primates have less and less space in which to live and find food. With fewer trees to hide in, they are at the mercy of hunters (who kill them for food or capture them to sell as pets, for research or to zoos). Tropical rain forests contain the greatest variety of plant and animal life on earth. Unfortunately, they are being destroyed (burned or cleared) at the rate of about 50 million acres (20 million hectares) per year. Scientists believe that, at this rate, almost all the earth's rain forests—together with the great diversity of plants and animals they support—will be gone in less than 200 years.

Clearing land for farms and towns, lumbering, mining, building dams and draining wetlands—all alter the environment to the detriment of the wildlife in the area. Pollution is another major environmental change that is killing off plants and animals at an alarming rate. Chemicals that are used to kill insects get into the food of some birds and cause them to lay eggs with weak shells or no shells at all. (Bald eagles and pelicans have been so affected.) Some species of fish are dying out because the ponds they live in are polluted by acid rain (rain that contains pollutants from the air). Industrial wastes dumped into lakes, seas and oceans have adversely affected marine life.

Of course, many animals are threatened with extinction because human beings kill them for food. The Hawaiian state bird (the nene—a type of goose) and several kinds of clams and fish caught in the U.S. are endangered because they are being overharvested. Many species have been hunted almost to the point of extinction because of their fur, hides, feathers or other parts. These include the big cats, crocodiles, egrets and birds of paradise. Elephants are killed for the ivory in their tusks, which are used to make ornamental carvings. Rhinoceroses are killed for their horns, which are used as medicine and in religious ceremonies. Recently, the World Conservation Union in Switzerland announced that there were only about 7,000 tigers left in the wild, most of them in India. Tigers are being killed off very rapidly because their bones, crushed and powdered, are a major ingredient in folk medicines used in China. Poachers can sell these tiger bones for as much as $170 a pound!

Intentionally and unintentionally, human beings are the cause of much plant and animal destruction. Now, however, as the article indicates, many organizations are fighting to maintain biological diversity by protecting endangered species. Many nations have signed agreements to save endangered species. National parks, zoos and groups of concerned citizens are also doing their part.

Animals Mentioned in the Article:

the badger: The badger is a rather small, nocturnal carnivore that belongs to the same family and order as the skunk and the weasel. Like the skunk, it has scent glands that it uses defensively. The adult badger is about 30 inches (76 cm) long and weighs about 25 pounds (11 kg). Its stiff fur has been used in brushes and as trim on coats and jackets.

the condor: A condor is a large, extremely rare bird. It is a vulture, which usually feeds on dead animals but sometimes attacks live prey. To save the California condor from extinction, in 1987 a rescue program was initiated. It involved taking eggs from nests and incubating them, then breeding the young birds. In 1987, the last California condor was captured. Now, to protect the species from extinction, all the condors live in captivity.

AUDIOVISUAL AIDS

Photographs of some of the animals being discussed would be helpful and interesting.

- The article is recorded on the audiocassettes accompanying the program.

READING SKILLS

Making Inferences: Have students reread paragraph 11 and make some inferences about Mr. Halle's attitude toward the California condor.

Scanning: Have students scan the article to look for reasons why the topic is timely (why it's in the news at this time). The answer is in paragraph 5.

Summarizing Ideas: Have students reread paragraphs 10 to 12, and then summarize Mr. Halle's moderate ideas in a few sentences.

WORD STUDY

Word Meanings:

- In paragraph 2, the author speaks of "tiger reserves." What does the word *reserves* mean here? Discuss the various meanings of the verb *reserve* and the noun *reservation.*
- The article uses both these phrases: *biological diversity* and *genetic diversity.* Point out that they have the same meaning.
- The word *ensure* is used in paragraph 8 and *ensuring* in paragraph 4. Discuss the meaning (to make sure, to guarantee).
- Have students look at paragraph 7, and discuss the meanings of "dummy humans" (not dumb humans!) and "mimicry."
- Have students contrast the meanings of *dangerous* and *endangered.*

GRAMMAR AND SENTENCE PATTERNS

Present and Past Participles as Adjectives: Endangered is a past participle used as an adjective. Point out that the meaning is that someone or something is causing the species to be in danger. What is the difference between *endangered* and *endangering?* Point out that in general, with the past participle the accompanying noun is acted on (animals are endangered by various factors); with the present participle the accompanying noun is doing the action (endangering factors for animals include the pollution and the loss of natural environments). Have students find an article in a newspaper that has several participles used as adjectives.

Got To: In colloquial English, *got to* is sometimes used to mean "must" or "have to." Paragraph 9 has an example. Americans sometimes say, "Gotta go now," meaning "I have (got) to leave."

STYLE AND TONE

Although this is a serious topic, the author played with the language he used and thereby inserted a note of humor. Ask students if anything about the article seemed funny to them. Three obviously funny spots are (l) the pun in the first paragraph (The expression *get off my back* means "stop bothering me or nagging me to do something." A tiger on one's back would be quite a bother!); (2) the first sentence of paragraph 13 (The idea is expressed in a humorous and memorable way); (3) the quotation from Jonathan Swift (the great eighteenth-century English satirist) in paragraph 13. (It may be necessary to explain *hath*, an old-fashioned form of has.)

EXTENDED ACTIVITIES

Letter Writing: For further information about efforts to save endangered species as well as practice in writing a business letter, each student can write to a zoo, national park, environmental organization or governmental body for the latest information about efforts to save endangered plants and animals.

Class Trip: A class trip to a zoo or animal reserve would tie in well with this reading.

Science and Environment: Article 2

Gallbladder Takes a Bow

BACKGROUND

The Gallbladder: After reading this article, students may wonder and worry about Karen Bennett. Why did she need to have her gallbladder removed? Will she be able to live a normal life without it? When the author quotes Karen, she always sounds cheerful and lighthearted about her experience. A look into the nature and effect of gallbladder surgery suggests that this is a reasonable response.

The gallbladder is a small, pear-shaped organ 3 to 4 inches long (7.5 to 10 cm) and about 1 inch wide (2.5 cm). It lies under the liver on the right side of the body. Its function is to store bile that is produced in the liver. This bile is then discharged after meals to aid in the digestion of fats.

Although the gallbladder is a useful organ, it sometimes becomes more trouble than it's worth. The gallbladder can cause a lot of pain when it produces gallstones that block a duct. Gallstones are created when the chemicals in the gallbladder get out of balance. In the United States, most gallstones are composed primarily of crystallized cholesterol; the rest are calcium salts of bile pigment. Among Americans, the development of gallstones is very common. About 1 in 10 Americans develop them. The condition is much more common among women and among people who are middle-aged or elderly. (Karen was not the typical patient.) Sometimes gallstones cause no problem. But if their presence causes pain, the usual treatment is removal of the gallbladder (a surgical procedure called cholecystectomy). If a gallbladder patient is young and in good health, surgery is usually recommended. It is a simple, safe procedure and the only way to guarantee that the problem will not recur. There are, however, other ways to get rid of gallstones, some of them still experimental.

Karen will get along just fine without her gallbladder. It is not vital to maintaining normal body functions because bile can be delivered directly from the liver into the duodenum.

Laparoscopy: The word part *-scope* refers to an instrument used to see something. *Laparo-* refers to the loin, flank or abdomen. A laparoscope is a type of endoscope (an instrument used to see inside the body).

The Appendix: This body organ, referred to in paragraph 31, is a small appendage of the large intestine. When it gets infected, it is surgically removed. In more general usage, the word *appendix* means an outgrowth or something added, for example, the appendix of a book.

Etiquette: The origin of the word *etiquette* is very interesting. In the seventeenth century, the French King Louis XIV gave everyone who entered his court *une etiquette* (a ticket). On it was written a list of rules of acceptable behavior while in his court. Today, *etiquette* means appropriate, polite manners. Sometimes, when Americans aren't sure about the best way to handle a social matter, they consult a book written by an expert in this field. Letitia Baldrige is such an expert. Notice that her book (mentioned in paragraph 5) is about good manners in the 90s. This suggests that, in the U.S. at least, what is considered acceptable can change with time.

Financial Planner: Karen's occupation is mentioned in paragraph 7. A financial planner helps clients find appropriate investments for their savings.

A Snack: In paragraph 1, Karen is putting out potato chips and popcorn for her guests. These are common snacks to serve guests in the United States. Popcorn is especially appropriate in this situation because Americans often buy it to eat during a movie at a theater.

AUDIOVISUAL AIDS

Get a drawing of the gallbladder and liver from a general or medical encyclopedia, and show it in class.

- The article is recorded on the audiocassettes accompanying the program.

READING SKILLS

The Headline: Discuss the figurative meaning of the headline. Then discuss situations in which a person might really take a bow (a literal use of the expression) and other situations in which the expression is used figuratively to mean that a person is given credit for doing a good job.

Paraphrasing: Have students reread paragraph 8, and then (without looking at the article) paraphrase Karen's feelings about watching the videotape. This is a good opportunity to introduce the word *ambivalent.* Students can then discuss actions that they have felt ambivalent about doing.

Making Inferences: Have students reread paragraph 31. Note Ms. Baldrige's dislike for "self-absorption." What does she consider good manners? Have students make inferences about this. (The answer: not talking much about yourself but showing an interest in others.)

WORD STUDY

Word Parts: Note the three word parts in the word *unconscious. Con-* means "with"; *-scious* means "knowledge"; *un-* means "not." Ask students if a person can be unconscious while still awake. Point out that a person can be awake and alert but not notice (not be conscious of) some particular event. But the same word (unconscious) is also used to describe a person who is totally unaware of anything happening. Karen is unconscious during her surgery because of the anesthesia she was given.

Pronunciation: Two common word parts often used in the field of medicine are *physio-* which means "nature," and *psycho-*, which means "mind." Remind students that the letters *ph* are pronounced [f], and that when a word begins with either *ps-* or *pn-*, the letter p is silent.

Colloquial English: Note the informal English in this reading: *kind of* (which means rather) and *gross* (both in paragraph 8). Discuss the meanings of these words in the contexts in which they are used.

Onomatopoeia: Point out that the adjective *whooshing* (in paragraph 26) is an onomatopoeic word, a word that imitates a sound. The word *whoosh* means a loud rushing noise that sounds like moving air or water.

GRAMMAR AND SENTENCE PATTERNS

Pronoun Reference: In paragraph 1, what claim does the pronoun *that* refer to? Ask students to paraphrase the claim and then tell why it's difficult to verify.

Indefinite Pronoun *One:* Remind students that, in paragraph 5, "one's surgery" means "a person's surgery." It refers to "any person." Compare it to the word *one* in paragraph 2, which is the number word.

EXTENDED ACTIVITIES

Class Discussion: Ask students to discuss, from their own hospitalizations or from visiting a patient, the ways in which TV shows and videotapes are used in hospitals today to entertain and to inform patients.

Parts of the Body: It is helpful for students to learn the names of the body parts, external and internal. Charts are a necessity for teaching the internal organs. The game "Simon Says" (in which students follow the commands of the leader, but only if he or she precedes the command with "Simon Says") is one entertaining way to review external body parts. These are examples of good commands to use:

"Touch your ankle. Put your fingertips on your shoulders. Put your thumb on your forehead. Stick out your tongue. Bend your right elbow. Put your index finger in front of your lips."

Science and Environment: Article 3

Dolphins Display Cunning and Brutality in Courtship

BACKGROUND

We thought that dolphins were friendly, intelligent, loyal, obedient and graceful. Now scientists are telling us that they're cruel, devious, conspiratorial, misogynous gang-bangers. Dolphins are often the star attractions at zoos, aquariums and aquatic theme parks. They jump on command through fiery hoops and in synchronization with other dolphins. They seem delighted to perform their tricks and sidle up to their human handlers, content with the applause of their audience, a pat on the head and a gift of some raw fish now and then. But dolphins have a darker side, as this article demonstrates.

In the article, we can find out about an unusual ability that dolphins have: to plot with others, communicate plans and execute them effectively. This indicates intelligence and communicative skills beyond what most other animals possess.

Dolphins, porpoises and whales are often thought of as fish since they live in the water. However, they are aquatic mammals. They cannot live indefinitely under water and must come to the surface periodically for air. They have "blowholes" at the top of their skulls to exhale air, even under water. Their young are born alive and are suckled by the parents.

Dolphins are born singly after a gestation period of about a year. At birth, they are about 3 feet (1 m) long and weigh about 26 pounds (12 kg). Bottle-nose dolphins, the largest and most popular of the species, grow to a length of about 6 feet (2 m) and weigh as much as 440 pounds (200 kg). Dolphins are sometimes confused with porpoises, which are smaller and do not have the characteristic snout of dolphins. Dolphins are found in all warm and temperate seas. There are even some fresh-water species.

Dolphins have been studied for many years because of their intelligence and their ability to communicate with other dolphins. They do this by emitting high-pitched, sometimes ultrasonic sounds. Scientists have been trying to develop a language of these sounds so that they can communicate with dolphins and understand them better. Dolphins also emit clicking sounds to detect objects in the water. This ability is similar to the sonar that bats use.

Explanation of Terms in the Article:

utopian-socialist manner (paragraph 2): This expression refers to a congenial society in which individuals cooperate with and assist other members of the group.

herding (paragraph 8): This word describes the collecting of individuals and small groups and bringing them together.

opportunistic (paragraph 14): This word suggests selfish behavior, using opportunities to one's own advantage.

Gray matter (paragraph 15): The brain is gray. The term is used in the article (and commonly) to mean intelligence.

soap opera effect (paragraph 15): Soap operas are radio or television shows that are highly charged stories of people's emotional lives. The characters exhibit jealousy and suspicion. Here, the soap opera effect refers to the constantly changing alliances between dolphins.

AUDIOVISUAL AIDS

Bring photographs to class to show students the animals mentioned in the article: dolphins, whales, chimpanzees, baboons and pandas.

READING SKILLS

Making Inferences: Have students discuss what general inferences they can make about dolphins or about animals in captivity, based upon this article. One answer: Perhaps animals behave differently in captivity than they do in the wild, where they can travel in large groups and roam freely.

Comprehension Check: Here are six questions to check student comprehension. Students can search for the answers individually, with partners or in small groups.

the headline and paragraph 25: When are dolphins most unkind to each other? (Answer: when they are seeking a mate)

paragraph 1: What three characteristics traditionally attributed to dolphins are mentioned here? (Answers: They're happy, playful and highly intelligent.) Which of these has further research disproved? (Answer: that they're always happy and playful)

paragraph 3: Does this paragraph imply that dolphin groups are more or less sophisticated and devious than human groups? (Answer: either less sophisticated or perhaps equal, but not more)

paragraphs 4 and 12: Both of these paragraphs make the same general statement about the complex social behavior of male dolphins. What is that behavior? (Answer: Two groups join together to attack a third.)

paragraphs 19 to 21: Discuss the evolutionary theory put forth here about why dolphins are now so smart. (Answer: The smarter ones survived in larger numbers. This is the theory of natural selection.)

paragraph 24: What are the dolphins really doing while they are "dawdling in a protected bay, nuzzling each other"? (Answer: The article strongly suggests that they are reaching a consensus—that is, considering until they come to an agreement about some group action.)

WORD STUDY

Homonyms: Paragraph 6 contains the plural noun *feats,* acts of skill. Point out that the singular—feat—and the plural noun *feet* are homonyms.

Word Parts: The word parts *syn-* and *sym-* mean "with" or "together." Discuss the meanings of these words from the reading: *synchrony* (paragraph 7) and *symphony* (paragraph 24). Compare these words to the familiar words *sympathy* and *sympathetic.*

GRAMMAR AND SENTENCE PATTERNS

Action Verbs: Paragraph 7 contains a number of action verbs that may be new words for students (somersault, bellyflop and so on). Have students make a list of all the verbs in the paragraph. Then demonstrate the meanings with gestures or simple drawings.

Adjectives with Negative Connotations: In this article, there are many adjectives that give negative descriptions of dolphins. Have students list these, and then discuss their meanings. If students list a word that is some other part of speech (for example, the noun *brutality*), have them look for the adjective form of the word (*brutal*) in a dictionary.

Pronoun Reference: Ask students the pronoun reference for the word *they,* which begins paragraph 4. (It is *researchers,* the first word in paragraph 3.) Point out that pronouns are not usually so far from the antecedents that they refer to.

EXTENDED ACTIVITY

Nature Film: Show a nature film. Have students discuss what they learned about animal behavior from seeing the film and what surprised them.

Flipper Films: In the 1960s, three American movies were made about a dolphin named Flipper, who was adopted by a human family. (The films were *Flipper, Flipper's New Adventure,* and *Flipper's Odyssey.* All are now available on videocassette.) Students might enjoy watching one of these, which present a real trained dolphin in action and show the dolphin as a gentle, intelligent creature.

Visit to a Zoo or Sea World Park: If there is a zoo or park nearby that has a trained dolphin show, plan a group trip there. Try to arrange in advance for one of the animal trainers to talk informally with your class after the show.

Science and Environment: Article 4

The Latest Riddle of the Sphinx

BACKGROUND

In October of 1992, a major earthquake hit Cairo, Egypt. People the world over were saddened to hear of the hundreds of people killed and the thousands injured and left homeless. But there was also a sigh of collective relief when inspectors announced that neither the Great Pyramids nor the Great Sphinx suffered substantial damage. If the Sphinx was built near the pyramids in order to protect the "divine" rulers buried nearby, then it has certainly done its job. But, if Robert Schoch (the geologist whose research is discussed in this article) is correct, then the Sphinx was built thousands of years before the pyramids.

Perhaps the site for the pyramids was selected by the ancient pharaohs because the Sphinx was there to serve as guardian. At any rate, the pyramids near the Great Sphinx are the largest of some 35 pyramids still standing in Egypt.

The Sphinx: The name *sphinx* almost certainly comes from an Egyptian word meaning living image. But in Greek, the word means an imaginary evil monster.

Why did the Egyptians choose to combine the human figure with a lion? To Egyptians, the lion symbolized great strength and protection. Representations of lions appeared often in Egyptian homes. For example, replicas of lions' paws commonly decorated the feet of chairs. When an Egyptian king went into battle, a tame lion often went beside him. The lion represented protection given by the king, but it also represented the god Horus, and, as such, was a protector of the king.

When the Great Sphinx is photographed alone, without any people in the picture, it is difficult to imagine its huge size. The body, including the outstretched paws and encircling tail, is about 240 feet (73 meters) long. Its height is about 66 feet (20 meters). The nose (now missing because of soldiers who shot at it for target practice) was about the size of the average Egyptian. Its head and body were carved directly out of a giant limestone rock. Stone blocks were put together to form its paws and legs.

The Great Sphinx stands in a desert near the west bank of the Nile River. It has been attacked by sand, wind, rain and sun, and all of these natural forces have worn away parts of it. Many times, the Sphinx was buried up to its neck in sand. According to one story, King Thutmose IV of Egypt cleared the sand away in the 1400s B.C., after he had a dream in which the god Horus asked him to do this. In the past two centuries, the sand has been cleared away at least four times. Today, the entire figure is unburied. In the 1970s, scientists began efforts to keep the stone from crumbling by treating it with chemicals. The problem of crumbling has been attributed to everything from road vibrations to rising water tables.

The Pyramids: At Giza, on the west bank of the Nile, there are ten pyramids, including the three largest and best preserved. These are called the Great Pyramids. They are the largest and most famous stone structures in the world. They are also the only survivors of the Seven Wonders of the Ancient World.

Time, nature and human attack have all tried unsuccessfully to destroy the Great Pyramids. The largest pyramid lost its top. The steplike sides of all three have been damaged by treasure hunters and by quarriers needing building stone. Yet, unless a viewer is standing very close, the eye fills in what's missing, and the pyramids retain their original basic design. The largest pyramid was made of more than 2 million stone blocks that weighed an average of 2.5 short tons (2.3 metric tons) each. Originally 481 feet (147 meters) high, it now stands about 450 feet (140 meters). Its base covers about 13 acres (5 hectares), an area large enough to hold 10 football fields.

Jericho: The city of Jericho (mentioned in paragraph 10) is located 6 miles (10 kilometers) north of the Dead Sea in the West Bank region of Palestine. Once part of Jordan, it became part of Israel after the 1967 Six-Day War.

Excavations there have uncovered remains of the oldest city yet discovered. Earliest remains date back to about 9000 B.C. The city was greatly expanded in approximately 8000 B.C. (the 9th millennium). A high wall was built around it and, on one side, a round tower 23 feet (7 meters) high with a flight of stairs inside. According to the Bible, the Israelites (under Joshua's leadership) shouted and blew their trumpets so loudly that the walls fell down. Today, tourists can see the ruins of this ancient wall.

RELATED READINGS

Additional Readings: Books about the treasures found in King Tut's tomb would tie in with a study of ancient Egypt. Tutankhamen was pharaoh from about 1347 to 1335 B.C. Desmond Stewart's *The Pyramids and the Sphinx* (Newsweek Book Division, 1971) is recommended for its fine text and beautiful color illustrations.

READING SKILLS

B.C. and A.D.: To understand the reading, students must realize that B.C. means before the birth of Christ or before the Common Era. Therefore, 5000 B.C. is earlier than 2500 B.C. (See paragraph 2.) Point out that years marked A.D. (which stands for *anno domini,* "in the year of our Lord" in Latin) or years not followed by any letters are counted from the year one (supposedly the year that Christ was born). Therefore, 5000 A.D. would be later than 2500 A.D.

Making Inferences: Have students reread paragraph 10 and decide whether the evidence in this paragraph supports Schoch or Lehner. In paragraph 14, Schoch says that it is "a reasonable hypothesis" that Pharaoh Khafre did not order the building of the Sphinx (paragraph 2) but merely ordered its repair and completion. Ask students if Schoch is sure that's what happened, or is he making an educated guess? Also, why might Schoch want to connect the Great Sphinx with Pharaoh Khafre at all? Is he trying to make other scholars (such as Lehner) less hostile toward his theories?

In general, what does this article suggest about our knowledge of the past? Why do history books need to be revised from time to time? (The past doesn't change, but what we know about it certainly does, primarily because of new evidence and new technology.)

WORD STUDY

Academic Fields: Discuss the difference between the fields of geology and archaeology. Why would specialists in both fields be interested in the Great Sphinx?

The Word *Great:* *Great* sometimes implies very large size and sometimes very high quality. Discuss the word's meaning in the phrases *the Great Sphinx* and *the Great Pyramids.*

Homonyms: In paragraph 5, the word *site* is used. Define it and its homonyms, *sight* and *cite.*

Similar and Identical: In paragraph 12, both these words are used. Ask students the difference between *very similar* and *identical.*

GRAMMAR AND SENTENCE PATTERNS

Passive Voice: The passive voice is used often in this article. Ask students why they think it is needed here. (The main reason is that we don't know the doer of the action, the builder of the Sphinx.) Have them locate various passive voice verbs in the article and identify the tense.

Two Meanings of *Since:* In paragraph 15, *since* is used twice. Ask students the following:

In which place does it mean "because"? In which place does it mean "from the time that"? In paragraph 17, which meaning does *since* have?

EXTENDED ACTIVITIES

Ancient Cultures Investigation: Have students give reports on various ancient cultures. Students interested in engineering could research how the Great Pyramids or the Great Sphinx were built. Those interested in art could report on the kinds of items found inside Egyptian tombs. Other topics might be ancient religions, ancient myths or the Seven Wonders of the Ancient World. Students interested in the Western Hemisphere could compare and contrast Peruvian or Central American pyramids with Egyptian ones. Students interested in the Far East might report about ancient civilizations there.

Geometric Shapes: Have students look in a dictionary or encyclopedia so that they can draw and define some common two-dimensional (square, rectangle, triangle, circle and so on) and three-dimensional shapes (cube, sphere, cone, pyramid and so on).

SECTION 7: SPORTS

Sports: Article I

A Chinese Tennis Player's Uneasy Season

BACKGROUND

Tennis and Tiananmen Square seem worlds apart—but not in the life of Chinese tennis pro, Hu Na. This article discusses the personal conflict that can occur when political concerns interfere with professional achievement.

The events in Tiananmen Square in Beijing took place in the spring of 1989, when Chinese students carrying banners of their schools assembled to press the Chinese government for more freedoms. Tiananmen Square has historically been the place where such protests occur. In fact, seventy years before the events that form the background of this article, students had gathered there to petition the government for the freedom of speech and the right to assemble. The 1917 protest, joined by merchants and workers as well, ended in success. The 1989 demonstration ended in death and imprisonment for some of the protesters.

Tiananmen Square is the 90-acre square entrance to the Forbidden City. In this square is a gigantic monument to Chinese revolutionary martyrs as well as the mausoleum of Mao Zedong, the original leader of communist China. Originally built in the 1420s during the Ming Dynasty, the square is now bordered by government buildings, Beijing's largest hotels and smaller stores and offices. It is similar to Washington, D.C.'s Mall.

Hu Na was one of millions of viewers watching footage of the confrontation of students and tanks on June 3, 1989. What we learn about her reaction is limited to her fears about her native city, Chengdu, and her inability to communicate with her parents there.

History of Tennis: Tennis began in France as a sport called *jeu de paume* or "game of the palm" several hundred years before Tiananmen Square was built. In the 1100s and 1200s, players used the palm of their hands to bat a ball over a net. In 1873, a game closely resembling the modern sport was introduced in England. At that time, tennis was played on grass, thus the name lawn tennis. The sport soon became even more popular than croquet in England, where the first major tennis tournament was played at Wimbledon in 1877. Today the sport has spread worldwide, and 100 countries now belong to the International Tennis Federation. Britain, France, Australia and the U.S. host the four major tennis tournaments. Still, most of the world's tennis players are amateurs, who take to the courts on weekends in the traditional white clothing of the sport.

RELATED READINGS

Articles in the Text: To discuss the idea of working under difficulty or duress, students might be asked to compare this article with the more humorous "Moscow Chefs: Where's the Beef?" in the Education section.

Items in the News: Students might clip articles that follow up on events in China since Tiananmen Square, as well as tennis articles for a discussion in class.

AUDIOVISUAL AIDS

- A map of Beijing with Tiananmen Square can be used in class. On other maps, students might locate the other major places mentioned in the article: Chengdu; San Diego; Newport, Rhode Island; and Schenectady, New York.
- Several documentaries have been made about the events in China in 1989. One might be shown in class.
- There are numerous sports videos on tennis—both on how to play the game and on particular matches. Show one of these in class.

READING SKILLS

Contrasting Details: Have students list in one category Hu Na's comments about playing tennis. Make a second category for her comments about the events in China.

Chronology: Have students make a list of events in Hu Na's personal and professional life in chronological order, giving years where possible.

WORD STUDY

Prefixes: The prefix *un-* means "not" or "contrary to." In the first paragraph, point out the prefix in the words *unknown* and *unseen.* Notice that if the element following *un-*

begins with a capital letter, it is separated with a hyphen, as in *un-American.* Another meaning of the prefix *un-* is to "reverse an action," as in *unlock.* (He will unlock the old gate with the new key.) A further meaning is to "release or remove from," as in *unearth.* (Scientists unearthed some ancient objects in their dig.)

NUMBERS AND MEASUREMENTS

Notice the *-th* ending on *90th* in paragraph 9. It is an ending for ordinal numbers. While the first three ordinal numbers use *-st* (1st or first), *-nd* (2nd or second) or *-rd* (3rd or third), numbers beginning with 4 use the *-th* ending (4th or fourth).

EXTENDED ACTIVITIES

Interview: Have students interview a person living in a foreign country about his or her current profession or life situation and how it is affected by news about "home."

Report: Have interested students do a report on the history of Tiananmen Square.

Earnings in Sports: Hu Na's earnings in 1989 were $12,000. Is that a good amount for a sports pro? Have students do research on what the average pro earns in various sports. You may want them to choose sports discussed in other articles in the text: baseball, soccer, skiing, chess and basketball.

Sports: Article 2

In Europe, It's Still Diamonds in the Rough

BACKGROUND

Although popular legend has it that baseball, the United States' national sport, was "invented" in Cooperstown, New York, in 1839, books as early as 1744 refer to a children's game called "base-ball." Whenever it originated, it is certain that American baseball was imported from England and based on a game called rounders. In rounders, a batsman hits a ball that is thrown and then proceeds around one or more bases. In the early days of baseball, the bases were made of a variety of materials including stakes, canvas bags, milking stools and posts. Early names for this sport in the U.S. were goal ball, post ball, town ball, round ball, as well as the more colorful names of one, two or three old cats, depending on the number of bases used.

In the 1840s in the U.S., baseball's rules were standardized, but the rules differed from those in modern baseball. Runs, which are the number of times a player successfully crosses home plate, were called aces, and it took 21 aces to win. During the American Civil War, in the 1860s, baseball was played extensively by both sides in the conflict—the North and the South. A formal league called the National League developed shortly thereafter, and by 1882 the American League had begun. These two leagues are the highest-level professional organizations of baseball in the U.S. today.

To "farm" talent for major league baseball clubs, minor league clubs were established by 1877. Most American players first play in the minor leagues or get their start in college or high school baseball programs.

In 1947, professional baseball in the U.S. celebrated an important milestone when the first black player, the great Jackie Robinson of the Brooklyn Dodgers, played in the major leagues. Until then, there had been a separate "Negro" league, which produced such legendary players as pitcher Satchel Paige. Today, excellent players of every race and ethnicity are represented in the Hall of Fame, a baseball museum in Cooperstown, New York, which was dedicated in 1939.

Though baseball began in the United States, it is established firmly in other parts of the world. Countries including Japan, Canada, the Dominican Republic, Panama, Venezuela, Puerto Rico, Mexico and Cuba have hugely successful leagues. Established by missionaries to Japan in the late 1800s, baseball is avidly played in two professional leagues there and is the most popular college sport.

Baseball, which has been played as an exhibition sport in the Olympics since 1912, became a medal sport in 1992. It has made real gains in Europe since its introduction in Italy during World War II. While its popularity is increasing in Europe, as this article explains, baseball has not become a truly international sport like soccer, basketball, horse-racing or boxing. Still, fans all over the globe understand such colorful phrases as "grand slam" (a home run with the bases loaded) and "pinch hitter" (a batter who replaces another), and baseball greats such as Babe Ruth, Mickey Mantle, Hank Aaron and Roberto Clemente are well known in many places.

RELATED READINGS

Articles in the Text: Have students read "You Can't Play Soccer in the Suburbs" in the Opinion section. Discuss the issue of what is gained and lost when a sport spreads to a new culture.

Items in the News: Have students clip baseball stories and discuss them in class. You may want to focus on a particular aspect of baseball such as its international flavor, some of its renowned players, or the economics of baseball, including the huge contracts that players in the U.S. negotiate. How does this compare to or differ from other "national pastimes"? What, for instance, do the best soccer players in England earn?

AUDIOVISUAL AIDS

Rent a video about baseball and show it in class or show a baseball movie such as *Field of Dreams, The Natural, Bang the Drum Slowly* or *Bull Durham.*

READING SKILLS

Details: Have students choose one European country that is discussed in the article. Then have them keep track of what details that writer uses to characterize baseball's development in that country. Give each student a different country to "track" as he or she reads the article or to scan for if he or she has already read the article.

WORD STUDY

Dictionary Work: Have students look up and define the following words related to baseball: *pinch-hit, strikeout, homer, bullpen.*

Word Meanings: In paragraph 5, the writer refers to the biennial championships. Have students discuss the meanings of the words *annual, semiannual, biennial* and *perennial.*

Phonics and Pronunciation: Point out many words in the article that begin with the letter *c* having the *k* sound: *coach, catch, cultural, country, classes, Canadians, cousin* and *continental.* Remind students that the letter represents the *s* sound when it occurs before *e* or *i* (such as *ceiling* and *decide*).

STYLE AND TONE

Point out the view of the quality of baseball played in its European setting suggested by the word choice: Coach Daniels was "amazed" (paragraph 1). When the team took the field it was a "disaster" (paragraph 3). Is this tone maintained throughout, or do the words take on a more hopeful tone? Is it positive or negative that the article ends with the phrase "sport of miracles" (paragraph 24)? Is there a bias to the author's view of European baseball?

EXTENDED ACTIVITIES

Reports: Have students look in an encyclopedia for the biography of a famous baseball player. Have students present their biographies to the class.

Olympics: Have students share what they know about the Olympics: what sports are played, when they take place, famous Olympic stars and so on.

Sports: Article 3

Man Still Beats Chess Machine, for Now

BACKGROUND

It is thought that chess originated around the year 500 in what is now Pakistan. A Hindu game, its original name was *chaturanga.* From the region of Pakistan, chess spread to Persia (Iran) and picked up much of its terminology. For instance, the name chess itself is derived from the Persian word for king, *shah.* Checkmate, the victory of a player in chess, originally was *shah mat,* meaning "the king is dead." The Arabs, who conquered Persia in the seventh century, spread the game to Europe, where it was first played in Spain, Sicily and Constantinople. Chess as a modern game under its current rules existed by the 1700s, when François André Philidor was the first official European champion.

Though moves in chess are varied, certain strategies prevail. Since the white pieces always go first, the "white" player takes the initiative by occupying the central squares on the board. Each side tries to control the game in the fewest possible moves and to protect its men, especially the king. "Capturing" the king is the way to win the game. An occasional checkmate happens by surprise, but the game is usually won by force when one side, after losing many pieces, becomes defenseless against checkmate. A draw occurs when neither side has enough pieces for a checkmate to occur. A special kind of draw, called a stalemate, occurs when neither side can move its pieces to checkmate without exposing its own king.

Out of the play of chess, a lot of metaphors for victory, loss, and strategy have been derived. "I was a pawn (minor chess piece) in the game," says someone who's been used for the benefit of another. "Our argument ended in a stalemate," a person says, claiming that neither side has won a hotly contested debate or discussion.

Though chess and its language have a long history, computer chess was not played until 1958. Since then, programmers have shown great interest in developing a computer chess program. They see it as a model for the human decision-making process. One of the first serious computer chess programs, Mac Hack, was developed in 1966 at the Massachusetts Institute of Technology. The program discussed in this article, Deep Thought, created publicity for computer chess when it tied for first in a high-level tournament. But it was another program, Hitech, created at Carnegie-Mellon University in Pittsburgh, Pennsylvania, that first outscored a grandmaster. Because new chess computers are being programmed with the ability to access and store materials by player, score, opening variation and event, it is possible that grandmasters like Mr. Kasparov will routinely be checkmated by computers in the future.

RELATED READINGS

Articles in the Text: Have students read "New Under the Tree: Computers for Tots" in the Education section for a discussion of the expanding applications of computers in our lives. Have students offer their opinions of technological innovations such as computer chess.

Items in the News: Have students clip news stories about chess and new computer applications for discussion in class.

AUDIOVISUAL AIDS

- Bring a chess game to class or have a student do so. Discuss the different pieces that are used. If several people in the class know how to play chess, have classmates observe a game.
- There are inexpensive computerized chess games now used for entertainment. If anyone owns such a game, bring it to class to demonstrate a game of computerized chess.
- The article is recorded on the audiocassettes accompanying the program.

READING SKILLS

Making Predictions: This article poses a central question: Is the era of human chess supremacy drawing to a close? Using what students have read here and their own opinions about computers in chess, have them answer the question. What are the reasons for their answers?

Scanning: Have students scan the article for the answers to these questions: (1) Who is Bent Larsen? (2) Who is Murray Campbell ? (3) How much money did Kasparov earn for playing Deep Thought? (4) The makers of Deep Thought are planning another computer that may be ready in five years. How many positions a second will it be able to scan?

WORD STUDY

Using Adverbs: Point out the frequent use of adverbs (*-ly* words) in this article to provide "color" for verbs: *handily* (paragraph 1), *rapidly* (paragraph 4), *mildly* (paragraph 5), *seriously* (paragraph 9), *carefully* and *precisely* (paragraph 14) and *decisively* (paragraph 17).

Parts of Speech: Students might be asked to turn the adverbs into adjectives (*handy, rapid, mild, serious, careful, precise, decisive*) or nouns (*handiness, rapidity, mildness, seriousness, carefulness, precision,* and *decisiveness.*)

GRAMMAR AND SENTENCE PATTERNS

Subject/Verb Agreement: Notice that the subject pronoun *none* (see paragraph 11) usually takes a singular verb: "None of the five is . . . a strong chess player." This is because *none* takes the meaning of "not one" or "no one." However, when *none* can be construed as standing for a group of people or things, it takes a plural verb: "None were more unhappy than people who lost in the first round." However, the first use is more common, and generally, *none* takes a singular verb.

STYLE AND TONE

Kasparov and the author personify (give human qualities to) Deep Thought. Notice the characterizations of Deep Thought as *intimidated* (paragraph 17) and *frightened* (paragraph 19).

EXTENDED ACTIVITIES

Class Visit: Is there a place in your city where people gather to play chess? Take a trip to observe a chess game being played, or have a chess expert come to lecture the class about chess. Ask for this person's opinion about developments in computer chess. Ask for explanations of chess terms in the article.

Computer Fair: Have students report about the use of computers in their everyday lives. What do computers do for them? What would they like computers to do for them?

Sports: Article 4

Downhill Racers: Taking On the Mountain at Any Risk

BACKGROUND

Skis over 4,000 years old have been found in excavated bogs in Scandinavia, where skiing is thought to have begun. It is also known that the early Laplanders were skiers. Imagine the sight at the Battle of Oslo in 1200, of Norwegian troops on skis. Early skiing was usually done for practical reasons—for warfare or for transportation. It was not until 1862 that the first ski competition was held in Oslo, Norway, and it took until our century for skiing to catch on as a popular sport.

The equipment needed for skiing has also changed tremendously. Skis as short as 3 feet (1 meter) were used in early warfare. Today, skis are long, flat runners made of wood, plastic or metal. All are arched, or "cambered," in the middle and are built for flexibility and resilience. Ski poles of metal or fiberglass, which reach a skier's waist, are used for downhill skiing. Boots, bindings and parkas have also gone "high-tech," with safety, lightweightness and wind- and water-resistance factors that are precisely calculated.

Four million skiers participate in the sport in the United States, and the number continues to grow. New ski slopes, many of them with artificial snow, continue to open and expand skiing to areas where it had earlier been impossible. Enthusiasm for skiing has also grown in South America, Japan and parts of southern Europe, where skiing had traditionally been less popular than in the Scandinavian countries.

The sport today divides into two branches, Nordic skiing, which consists of cross-country events and the ski jump, and Alpine skiing, which consists of downhill and slalom racing. The champion skiers in the article we are discussing, then, are engaging in the challenging sport of Alpine skiing. While the casual skier's goal is to enjoy the run and reach the destination safely, speed and control are the goals of the downhill racer. Skiers race one at a time with their speeds measured against one another. Because snow conditions may vary, record times are not considered primary to the sport as they are in track or swimming events.

Top Alpine skiers compete in the Winter Olympics and for the World Cup, which is awarded annually on the basis of points in international competition. Everyone agrees that skiing is one of the most exhilarating and risky competitive sports. However, because of the conditions and remoteness of the most challenging ski runs, it does not enjoy the wide audience of many other sports.

RELATED READINGS

Items in the News: Have students clip articles about skiing to discuss in class. Also, students might be encouraged to bring in articles about other dangerous sports: sky diving, boxing, car racing and so on.

AUDIOVISUAL AIDS

- If available, bring in a pair of skis or other skiing equipment. Another possibility would be a catalogue of skiing equipment and outerwear.
- There are also videos of the Winter Olympics and other skiing events. Bring them to class for students to view and discuss.
- The article is recorded on the audiocassettes accompanying the program.

READING SKILLS

Main Ideas: Have students reread the article and discuss the positive and negative aspects of fear in downhill skiing. Glamour, skill, confidence and courage are also terms that students might discuss, as well as the contrast between nervousness and fear.

Interviews: Many people were interviewed for the article and are quoted. Students might make a chart of the names of skiers and what they have to say about their experience with the sport. Do they mostly agree? Do any differ? Another possibility would be to categorize the quotes under the main idea headings of fear, glamour, skill, confidence and courage.

WORD STUDY

Suffixes: The *-er* suffix is often added to a verb to name one who participates in an activity. This article mentions readers, writers and skiers. But not all verbs add *-er* to form "participant" nouns. Those who coach are coaches, for instance. Also, for "participant" nouns formed from parts of speech other than verbs, the endings vary. Those who participate in the Olympics (noun) are *Olympians.* Those who are *enthusiastic* (adj.) about a sport are *enthusiasts.* Have students list more *-er* nouns (teacher, worker, sleeper, complainer, viewer and so on). Note, too, that some participant nouns add *-or,* such as *orator* and *sailor.*

Derivations: Some terms in skiing have interesting derivations. An Austrian term for short, connected parallel turns in skiing is the *wedeln.* A method of skiing using parallel skis, weight shifts and body rotation is called the "Christiana" or "Christie." Have students find the origin of these or other skiing terms.

STYLE AND TONE

Colorful Language: Notice how sports descriptions often involve metaphors relating to a skier's actions or accomplishments. In fact, sports writing is the area in which some of the most colorful news writing is found. Skiers *throw [themselves] down a mountain* (paragraph 2); they *go to the limit* (paragraph 4); one skier's concentration *flipped* (paragraph 17).

EXTENDED ACTIVITIES

Guest Speaker: Have an experienced skier come to class and discuss his or her experiences.

Economics of Skiing: If possible, have students investigate the cost of skiing in your area (price of buying or renting ski equipment, ski lessons and so on). Have students compare results and draw conclusions. How does skiing compare with other sports?

Answers to the Student Text Exercises

Note: The answers for the first exercise in *Getting the Message* are in the student text, in the section at the back titled *Comprehension Check*. This allows students to get immediate feedback on how well they understood the article.

SECTION 1: NEWS

News: Article 1

Smokers Under 18 in Iowa Now Outlaws

II. Expanding Your Vocabulary
Getting Meaning from Context

1. a	4. b	7. a
2. b	5. a	8. a
3. b	6. a	9. a

III. Working with Idioms

1. Anyone under 18 can be caught smoking. The police can catch teenagers smoking and fine them for disobeying the law.
2. The law against smoking shares a spot with handling a cat stuck in a tree because both are not very important priorities for the police, who have more serious matters to handle.
3. Although the police have the option to arrest teens, many will choose not to do so.
4. The police are not too keen, or enthusiastic, about the law. Some believe that the law will not stop teenagers from smoking.

IV. Analyzing Paragraphs
Sample Answers
10, Mr. Coverdale, for, "Cigarettes are the gateway to other drugs that are illegal"
12, Wendy Spuehler, against, "It's stupid"
14, Lieutenant Michael C. Hammes, against, would not "scare many kids" away from cigarettes
Sentences will vary.

News: Article 2

Should ID's Be Required? Dutch Agonize

II. Expanding Your Vocabulary
A. Getting Meaning from Context

1. b	4. a	7. b
2. a	5. b	8. a
3. a	6. b	

B. Reading for Suggested Meanings

1. The word *incompatible* means that the law does not fit in with the country's democratic traditions. This is because the law could limit people's freedoms and make it easier for government to monitor and control the actions of citizens.

2. *Arbitrarily* means that the police can stop anyone at random at any time and that this exercise of power is not checked or limited.
3. *Tight* controls are very strict, rigid ones. People who are concerned with individual rights would want to limit the situations in which police can stop people and ask them to show identification.

III. Working with Idioms

1. ruled out
2. suffered a setback
3. go ahead with
4. create a headache

IV. Analyzing Paragraphs

1. Police can stop people on the street and ask for identity cards arbitrarily. This can lead to discrimination against certain groups.
2. The national identity card could help the government eliminate "work black," in which people do not report earnings to tax authorities. This is because tighter controls could be established for workers.
3. Paragraphs 10 and 11 present an argument for the law. They point out that a mandatory national identity card would help the police, who are often forced to release people they arrest for minor crimes because they cannot establish the identity of these people.

News: Article 3

EC Sets 'Ecolabel' for Green Products

II. Expanding Your Vocabulary

A. Getting Meaning from Context

1. a	4. b	7. b
2. a	5. b	8. b
3. a	6. a	

B. Matching Opposites

6 required
3 decide not to do
5 honest, truthful
7 partly
1 harm, damage
4 very few of
2 consumer

C. Practicing Useful Vocabulary

1. implement
2. consumer, spurious
3. plethora

III. Making Sense of Sentences

Sample Answers

1. Companies whose ecological claims are false may not qualify to receive ecolabels.
2. A manufacturer whose products are ecologically friendly will meet the criteria to receive an ecolabel.
3. A consumer whose washing machine is too old to fix should seek to buy a new machine with an ecolabel.
4. A spokesman whose company markets products in Europe said that a single ecolabel has many advantages.
5. A product whose materials are dangerous to the environment is not likely to earn an ecolabel.

News: Article 4

A Rain of Protest on Columbus's Parade

II. Expanding Your Vocabulary

Getting Meaning from Context

1. b	4. a	7. a
2. b	5. b	8. a
3. a	6. b	9. b

III. Working with Idioms

1. *Hoopla* is noisy, excited activity. American Indians say that civilization began in North America long before the arrival of Columbus and so they question why there is so much attention given to Columbus. Also, they believe that the arrival of Columbus helped to signal the start of the destruction of their civilization.
2. The Italian-Americans feel they have gotten a bad deal and that their motives for organizing Columbus Day celebrations are misunderstood. They feel that the holiday is for all ethnic groups and they do not intend to be negative toward any group.
3. The American Indians want to pass on their culture and language to the next generation. They do not want their culture to die out.
4. The Europeans have a high opinion of Columbus. The American Indians, however, do not. They feel that their civilization existed before Columbus and that his arrival led to its disappearance.

IV. Focusing on Style and Tone

Positive: hero, honor, tribute, discoverer

Negative: genocide, scapegoat, hoopla, betrayal

Additional sets of words will vary.

SECTION 2: OPINION

Opinion: Article 1

You Can't Learn Soccer in the Suburbs

II. Expanding Your Vocabulary

Getting Meaning from Context

1. b	4. a	7. b
2. a	5. b	8. b
3. a	6. b	

III. Working with Idioms

1. According to the author, people should raise a glass to Ted Turner (give him credit and thanks) because his cable TV service is broadcasting the World Cup competition while nonpay TV is not.
2. The author's sticking point in praising the United States is its indifference to soccer. It is the one thing that he can't praise about the United States.
3. The way a team plays soccer reveals what is happening in its society. For example, as Brazil has tried to become an economic power, the quality and excitement of its soccer team have declined.
4. The author has love for soccer in his bones because he grew up playing it and enjoying it, and it has remained a part of his life.

IV. Analyzing Paragraphs

1. To show their interest in soccer, Americans would mention that millions of children play soccer and that the United States has a new, young team representing it in the World Cup competition.
2. The author thinks that soccer must be played by kids on the street, not in

organized teams playing on perfect fields. He is maintaining that soccer is a popular game, a game to be played by anyone.

Opinion: Article 2

An Economics Lesson at the Barbershop

II. Expanding Your Vocabulary

Getting Meaning from Context

1. a	4. b	7. a
2. a	5. b	8. a
3. b	6. a	9. a

III. Working with Idioms

1. the hustle and bustle, catch up on
2. state-of-the-art, spanking new
3. get it over with
4. the cornerstone of

IV. Analyzing Paragraphs

1. Paragraphs 1 to 5 introduce the nature of the Japanese barbershop as a place where people can go to relax, escape from the hustle and bustle of everyday life and receive good service.
2. His new shop is very modern. His prices are much higher now than in the past.
3. Mrs. Tanaka shampoos and massages while Mr. Tanaka cuts hair. Mrs. Tanaka also shaves customers.
4. The author suggests that foreign businesspeople can learn the importance of excellent service from the example of the Japanese barbershop.

Opinion: Article 3

Much Ado About Mozart: Craze Leaves Expert 'Astounded'

II. Expanding Your Vocabulary

A. Getting Meaning from Context

1. b	4. a	7. b
2. a	5. a	8. b
3. b	6. a	9. a

B. Practicing Useful Vocabulary

1. generated	5. appeals
2. astounded	6. fanatic
3. phenomenon	7. innovator
4. myth	

III. Working with Idioms

1. At the time the article was written, the bicentennial of Mozart's death was being commemorated. As a result, there was much attention to Mozart in the media.
2. By latching on to Mozart and associating themselves with the interest in Mozart by publishing articles on him, the magazines have contributed to the Mozart craze.
3. Since the Linz Symphony is long, a person would have to work hard for a long period just to copy it.
4. As people publicize Mozart, they are also giving publicity to other composers of the time, such as Haydn, and are creating interest in classical music in general.

IV. Focusing on Style and Tone

1. *Answers will vary. Students can choose any of the questions in the article (marked by Q).*
2. *Answers will vary.*

Opinion: Article 4

National Cliché or Good Metaphor?

I. Getting the Message

B. Germany, symphony; France, a perfectionist in a vineyard; Mexico, fiesta; Italy, opera; Spain, bullfight; United States, football; Belgium, lace

II. Expanding Your Vocabulary

A. Getting Meaning from Context

1. b	4. a	7. b
2. a	5. b	8. b
3. b	6. a	

B. Reading for Suggested Meanings

1. The word *metaphor* is more positive than *cliché,* which suggests an expression that is overused.
2. The example shows that the French are perfectionists, and that by touching the apple, the person is spoiling the perfect picture.
3. *Huddling* shows that Americans can get together on a problem, work hard to come up with a solution, and then go off on their own. When football players huddle, they talk about what the next play is going to be and coordinate their actions.

C. Working with Abstract Nouns

1. efficiency
2. aggressiveness
3. individualism
4. conformity
5. rigidity

III. Analyzing Paragraphs

1. Paragraphs 1 through 4 contrast the differences between Germans and Irish-Americans while eating. The Irish-Americans talk while eating; food is not as important as the conversation. The Germans do not talk much while they are eating meals.
2. The example in paragraphs 1 to 4 leads to the statement that people act in certain ways because they are members of a particular society.
3. Gannon believed that he had found a way to describe the differences in behaviors by metaphor, and he studied ways to characterize different societies.
4. anthropologists, organizational theorists
5. The German metaphor is probably discussed for so many paragraphs because the article began by talking about the behavior of Gannon's German wife. So these paragraphs continue the discussion of German culture.
6. The article does not have a conclusion. The article is written so that the background and general conclusions are stated in the middle paragraphs. Ending with an example continues to illustrate the points already made. Such an organization is not unusual in newspapers since later paragraphs in an article may have to be cut for reasons of space.

Opinion: Article 5

Hold Your Nose at the Steak House

II. Expanding Your Vocabulary

A. Getting Meaning from Context

1. b	4. a	7. a
2. a	5. b	8. b
3. a	6. a	9. a

B. Defining Useful Vocabulary

6 right to use
4 something given with nothing received in return
3 using up, eating
1 assist by giving money or financial favors
7 particular area where a kind of animal lives
2 not having enough to eat
5 gloomy, depressing
8 open lands where cattle are raised

C. Practicing Useful Vocabulary

1. consumption, undernutrition
2. subsidize, access, giveaway
3. grim

III. Analyzing Paragraphs

a third of the world's total grain harvest (consumed by cattle and other livestock)

400 million people (additional people who could be fed if land used for livestock were changed to grow grain for humans)

$45 million on advertising (money spent by the Department of Agriculture in a year to convince Americans to eat more beef) *Additional answers will vary.*

SECTION 3: BUSINESS

Business: Article I

Sociology of the Kimono: Everything Old Is Young

I. Getting the Message

B.

1. N	4. N	7. N
2. B	5. N	8. N
3. T	6. T	

II. Expanding Your Vocabulary

Getting Meaning from Context

1. a	4. a	7. a
2. b	5. a	8. a
3. a	6. b	9. b

III. Working with Idioms

1. It is not always apparent to the Western eye (people from Western nations) that Japanese designers are preserving something of the line of the kimono in their contemporary clothing design.
2. It seems odd that schools to teach women how to put on kimonos are booming, or attracting many students, because the kimono is a traditional part of Japanese culture. Learning how to put on a kimono would seem to be something that is learned at home, as part of everyday life.
3. The paragraph suggests that not much of the old order remained after World War II and that there were major changes in the society.
4. The new kimono is ready-to-wear.

IV. Making Sense of Sentences

Sample Answers

1. Sueko Otsuka not only still runs a sewing school, but also her garments are still on sale.
2. The new kimono is not only lower in cost but also easier to clean.
3. Today kimonos are sold not only in department stores but also in shopping malls.

Business: Article 2

For Eskimo Artists Seeking Inspiration, Money Talks

I. Getting the Message

B.

l. T	4. T
2. N	5. T
3. N	

II. Expanding Your Vocabulary

Getting Meaning from Context

l. b	4. a	7. b
2. a	5. b	8. b
3. b	6. b	

III. Working with Idioms

1. With the video camera, a dealer can see exactly what a carving looks like and so can make a better estimate of what he or she can sell it for. So guesswork is eliminated.
2. Eskimo artists are branching out and using different materials for their art to meet the demands of the market.
3. The Eskimo artists banded together (cooperated) to get better prices for their work.
4. Answers will vary.
5. This article proves the saying *money talks* because Eskimo artists are changing their art to be able to sell more.

IV. Analyzing Paragraphs

l. comparing past and present
2. high technology and sophisticated marketing techniques
3. The purists see the introduction of marketing techniques as spoiling and corrupting traditional Eskimo art. They believe the inspiration for the art should come from the artist, not the person buying the art.
4. Eskimo artists are now selling their works at high prices.
5. use of woodblocks and lithography, use of stencils, use of pencils and crayons, introduction of impressionist and modern art styles

Business: Article 3

Anxiously, Some Everyday Russians Are Making Their Own Mark on the Economy

I. Getting the Message

B.

1 pensions
2 salary and dividends
3 profits from business

II. Expanding Your Vocabulary

Getting Meaning from Context

l. a	4. b	7. b
2. a	5. b	8. a
3. a	6. a	

III. Working with Idioms

1. With her dressmaking, Natasha is able to earn quite a bit of money, which helps her family survive the hard economic times.
2. No. Natasha started the business on her own initiative. She did not have to be pushed.
3. Answers will vary.
4. The family has now had to adapt to the changing situation; it is no longer assured of having enough money to get by. The family has done new things to earn money: Stepanov gets money from his shares in the cafeteria and Natasha earns money from dressmaking.

5. The suggestion is that people who work hard may now be able to earn more money. So the new order may be better than old in the long run.

IV. Focusing on Style and Tone

A. Finding the Interview in the Article

Sample Answers

1. Paragraph 17: How do you manage to get by on your salary?
2. Paragraph 21: Why do you live with your parents?
3. Paragraphs 21-22: Why did you start your dressmaking business?
4. Paragraph 30: Do you expect to stay where you are now living?

B. Showing instead of Telling

1. washing the car (4): The family has enough money to own a car.
2. bartering with veal (19): The family is trying to use all resources it has to have a better life, and meat is a resource many other people don't have.
3. purchasing the sewing machine (22): The family was willing to invest money in an object that had the potential to save money, and which Natasha then used to make money.

Business: Article 4

King of the Court: High-Tech, High-Price Sneakers

I. Getting the Message

B.

1. a pie-shaped graph
2. The graph looks like a basketball.
3. a. Nike
   b. 40%
4. a. Reebok
   b. 16%
5. Converse had 9% of total sales in 1990.
6. From the Sporting Goods Intelligence Newsletter

II. Expanding Your Vocabulary

A. Getting Meaning from Context

1. b	5. b	9. b
2. a	6. b	10. a
3. b	7. b	
4. a	8. b	

B. Working with Adjectives

1. lightweight leathers (2)
2. dazzling array of colors (2)
3. sophisticated cushioning devices (2)
4. popular basketball player (8)
5. large majority of these shoes (13)
6. stirring play in a pickup game (20)
7. inflatable bladder (24)

III. Analyzing Paragraphs

Sample Answers

Similarities:

Both Nike and Reebok spent about $130 million each on advertising

focus on marketing rather than manufacturing issues

have similar price ranges

incorporate "new technologies" into their shoes

Differences:

Nike signed Michael Jordan

focuses on improving cushioning without a bladder

Reebok appealed to average players

does not tie its shoe to a specific athlete

uses Pump technology, which has an inflatable bladder

SECTION 4: EDUCATION

Education: Article 1

New Under the Tree: Computers for Tots

I. Getting the Message

B.

1. animated figures
2. matching skills
3. creation of stories

II. Expanding Your Vocabulary

A. Getting Meaning from Context

1. a	4. b	7. a
2. a	5. b	8. b
3. b	6. a	

B. Reading for Suggested Meanings

1. The parents want their children to go to the very best schools so that the children can get off to a good start in life.
2. Rudimentary subjects are relatively simple. They include skills such as recognizing numbers.
3. a. Positive reinforcement is designed to make people feel good about what they are doing and the progress they are making.
   b. Yes. It gives an immediate, upbeat response to a correct answer.
4. a. A dirge is a kind of slow, sad music played at funerals.
   b. A wrong answer produces sad music to signal an incorrect response. Its use here probably exaggerates how sad the music accompanying an incorrect answer really is.

III. Working with Idioms

1. pick out, give an edge
2. take a dim view of, turned off to
3. grab the attention of

IV. Making Sense of Sentences

Sample Answers

Pro

1. The goal is to prepare children for school and help them do better in the classroom. (paragraph 12)
2. Another goal is to help children make friends with computers. (paragraph 13)

Anti

1. We have to recognize that computers are a fact of life, but I am concerned that these toys are putting too much pressure on children at too young an age. (paragraph 27)
2. There is an overemphasis on memorization of letters and numbers . . . [C]hildren who are not ready to gain those skills may become turned off to learning or convinced they are dumb. (paragraph 28)

Education: Article 2

Moscow Chefs: Where's the Beef?

I. Getting the Message

B.

1. The school doesn't have the ingredients it needs for students to prepare dishes because of food shortages in Moscow.
2. Students see models of foods. When there is some food, only the better students get to work with it.
3. The teaching is mostly theoretical, and students do not get first-hand experience in making food.

II. Expanding Your Vocabulary

Getting Meaning from Context

1. b	4. b	7. a
2. b	5. a	8. a
3. a	6. a	

III. Working with Idioms

1. Learning to cook by the book means following the recipes and instructions exactly. Here the double meaning is that students are only using the book, the written instructions—they do not get to use actual food.
2. The role of fat in frying is to even out the temperature between the meat and the pan.
3. Kitchen equipment, such as knives, stoves and potato-peeling machines are at the ready for whenever food appears. The students use this equipment in their cooking.
4. Klokune rises above the current problems by looking forward to the day when students will have actual food to work with.

IV. Analyzing Paragraphs

1. c	3. c
2. b	4. b

Education: Article 3

For Japanese, Cramming for Exams Starts Where the Cradle Leaves Off

I. Getting the Message

B. The student has to surrender his or her childhood to succeed. The child is forced to act like an adult and think primarily about succeeding. The focus of the child's life is on passing exams, not developing social skills or other necessary life skills.

II. Expanding Your Vocabulary

A. Getting Meaning from Context

1. a	4. b	7. b
2. b	5. a	
3. a	6. b	

B. Reading for Suggested Meanings

1. Cram means put in too much.
2. An obsession is something a person thinks about all the time.
3. a. anxiety
   b. Parents want their children to get ahead in the educational system, as it currently exists. They are afraid to risk the possibility that their children will fall behind.
4. Apparently, as more children pass the test, the test has to get harder so that it still works to find the very best students and eliminate the less able ones.

III. Working with Idioms

1. get ahead	4. left out
2. worked	5. cram
3. pick up	

IV. Focusing on Style and Tone

A. Appreciating Elements of Effective Style

1. a. We assume that Naoto is an adult worker because of his heavy schedule.
   b. Naoto is an 11-year-old student.
2. The statement that Naoto makes sounds like the statement that a college student or an adult would make, not a child.
3. The children in the class don't seem to be enjoying themselves; the class doesn't seem like fun.

B. Noting Negative Connotations

1. hell	4. cram
2. obsession	5. supplanting
3. relentless	

The author uses the negative words. This suggests he has a negative view of the jukus.

Education: Article 4

What's in a Gesture? Kids Need to Learn

I. Getting the Message

B.

1. N	4. V
2. V	5. N
3. N	6. N

II. Expanding Your Vocabulary

A. Getting Meaning from Context

1. b	4. b	7. b
2. b	5. b	8. a
3. a	6. a	

B. Using Negative Prefixes

1. in	5. non
2. un	6. un
3. mis	inability (lack of ability)
4. un	disability (handicap)

III. Making Sense of Sentences

Sample Answers

A. Writing Noun Clauses with *That*

Sample Answers

1. Dr. Nowicki probably hopes that teaching children how to act nonverbally will continue to have positive results.
2. The research described in this article showed that some children had trouble understanding nonverbal messages.

B. Writing Adjective Clauses with *That*

Sample Answers

1. Children that cannot communicate nonverbally tend to be unpopular.
2. The researchers used a test that measured children's ability to read nonverbal messages.

SECTION 5: ARTS AND LEISURE

Arts and Leisure: Article I

Food for Luck: New Year's Rituals

I. Getting the Message

B. long noodles; Japan; the longer the noodles, the longer and better the new year

pork; Germany; will not have to scratch for a living the way chickens do

black beans; Japan; symbolize hard work and diligence

green cabbage; United States; symbolizes money for the new year

II. Expanding Your Vocabulary

Getting Meaning from Context

1. a	4. a	7. a
2. a	5. b	8. b
3. b	6. a	

III. Working with Idioms

1. get off to a good start
2. scratch for a living
3. get ahead
4. it's worked
5. dish

IV. Making Sense of Sentences

Sample Answers

1. Vasilopita, a special bread, is eaten in Greece for New Year.
2. Herrings, a kind of fish, are eaten in America for a New Year of abundance.
3. In the southern United States, some people eat Hoppin' John, a casserole of rice and black-eyed peas.

Arts and Leisure: Article 2

Hey, Give Yourself a Break and Go Jump in a Hole

I. Getting the Message

B. Some companies require employees to take longer vacations; some companies are moving to eliminate the traditional Saturday workday; there are all sorts of new kinds of leisure activities, indoor ski resorts, all-night golf courses and scores of amusement parks.

II. Expanding Your Vocabulary

A. Getting Meaning from Context

1. b	4. b	7. a
2. b	5. a	8. b
3. b	6. a	

B. Reading for Suggested Meanings

1. Perching is an action that describes a bird at rest. Since birds fly, the word *perched* is appropriate for a person who is going to "fly" through the air in a sky dive.
2. *Workaholic* has a negative connotation. It suggests that the person works too much.
3. *Quasi English* means "similar to English." Often English names used by the Japanese are not in true idiomatic English, as it is spoken by English speakers.
4. Because the author was able to complete the dive and arrive at the exit platform, he still had all his pride. He didn't make a fool of himself.
5. The word *bout* suggests that the author found the experience with leisure tiring.

III. Working with Idioms

1. The author is having second thoughts about making the indoor sky dive. He is questioning whether it is a good idea to try to perform the dive.
2. Probably the author wants to back out of jumping because he feels a bit scared.
3. The amusement parks are pushing, or selling, exciting activities, such as taking a roller coaster ride.
4. The author's blood pressure is going crazy because the author has just performed a rather scary indoor sky dive. This suggests that the author's heart is beating very quickly because of the frightening experience.

IV. Focusing on Style and Tone

Sample Answers

indoor ski resorts, indoor mountain-climbing centers

Arts and Leisure: Article 3

Art, Photography, Copyright and the Law

I. Getting the Message

B.

1. R	4. R	7. R
2. K	5. K	8. I
3. K	6. I	

II. Expanding Your Vocabulary

A. Getting Meaning from Context

1. b	4. a	7. a	10. a
2. a	5. b	8. a	
3. a	6. b	9. b	

B. Finding Words That Don't Belong

appeal, damages, testified, case, trial, charges, court, sue, vs. (versus)

III. Working with Idioms

1. wunderkind
2. made a name for himself
3. ripped off
4. in the name of, draw the line
5. "Nothing is sacred to Koons"

IV. Making Sense of Sentences

8; who is a photographer in California; Rogers; 2

15; who produces a weekly photo column called the Point Reyes Family Album for a newspaper in Point Reyes, California; Rogers; 2

16; who can do this in the name of art; Koons; 1

19; who normally carve crucifixes and church sculptures; artisans; 1

25; who set the Paris art world on its ear at the turn of the century by placing a urinal in a major exhibition; Marcel Duchamp; 2

Arts and Leisure: Article 4

Is There a European Accent in Euro Disneyland?

I. Getting the Message

B. *Sample Answers*

1. close to Paris, within a two-hour flight of 320 million Europeans (so it has a large potential market); there is good transportation to the park, including new highways and an express railway
2. other theme parks in France have failed; some French intellectuals oppose the project

II. Expanding Your Vocabulary

A. Getting Meaning from Context

1. b	4. b	7. a
2. a	5. b	8. b
3. a	6. a	9. a

B. Reading for Suggested Meanings

1. b	3. a
2. b	4. b

III. Working with Idioms

1. A stingy person wouldn't want to spend the money to stay in a costly, opulent hotel.
2. *Answers will vary.*
3. A tourist can take an express train to get from Euro Disney to Paris very quickly.
4. Employees will shave off their mustaches to keep their jobs. Their jobs are more important to them than their mustaches.
5. Euro Disney is close to Paris.

IV. Getting the Message: Follow-up Article

1. Going Down	4. Going Up
2. Going Down	5. Not Discussed
3. Not Discussed	6. Going Down

V. Making Sense of Sentences

1. Attendance at Euro Disney has been high, but Euro Disney expects to lose money during its first year in operation.

2. While attendance at Euro Disney has been high, Euro Disney expects to lose money during its first year in operation.
3. Although attendance at Euro Disney has been high, Euro Disney expects to lose money during its first year in operation.
4. Attendance at Euro Disney has been high. Still Euro Disney expects to lose money during its first year in operation.

SECTION 6: SCIENCE AND ENVIRONMENT

Science and Environment: Article 1

Even the Palawan Stink Badger Has Its Defenders

I. Getting the Message

B.

1. an example of an animal that is threatened but that is not very attractive or endearing
2. an example of a species to which many resources were devoted to help it survive, perhaps too many resources
3. an example of how an unattractive animal plays an important role in the environment

II. Expanding Your Vocabulary

Getting Meaning from Context

1. a	4. a	7. b
2. b	5. b	8. b
3. b	6. a	

III. Working with Idioms

1. dig into their pockets
2. ad infinitum
3. set free
4. die out

IV. Analyzing Paragraphs

1. 4	3. 10
2. 11	4. 15

Sample Answer

One way to save a species is to breed it in captivity and then set it free in its natural environment.

Science and Environment: Article 2

Gallbladder Takes a Bow

I. Getting the Message

B. Videos of operations can help patients recuperate; it helps to make medicine less mysterious to the patient; it is comforting for patients and their friends to see what happens in an operation.

II. Expanding Your Vocabulary

A. Getting Meaning from Context

1. b	4. a	7. b
2. a	5. b	8. b
3. b	6. a	

B. Reading for Suggested Meanings

1. Authorities who are skeptical question the worth of showing videotapes of operations.
2. Baldrige is against the idea of showing videotapes of surgery. Her pauses indicate her displeasure.
3. The videotaping of operations is being compared to a kind of entertainment. So the word *genre,* which describes an art form, is appropriate.

4. Surgeons were afraid that the videotapes would show the mistakes they made.
5. The star is Karen's gallbladder.

C. Finding the Word That Doesn't Belong
1. navel
2. etiquette
3. curiosity
4. financial analyst
5. blob

III. Working with Idioms
1. look forward to
2. hit-or-miss
3. play-by-play
4. gross
5. remove the veil

IV. Focusing on Style and Tone
1. Ms. Baldrige is against showing videotapes of surgery to other people at parties. The physicians quoted are in support of videotaping, saying that it can be comforting and helpful to patients and their friends.
2. The author is comparing the operation to a film or TV show. The comparison is appropriate because the operation is on videotape.

Science and Environment: Article 3

Dolphins Display Cunning and Brutality in Courtship

I. Getting the Message
B.

1. F	4. N
2. C	5. N
3. C	

II. Expanding Your Vocabulary
Getting Meaning from Context

1. a	4. a	7. b
2. b	5. a	8. a
3. b	6. b	

III. Working with Idioms
1. get away with
2. turned out, gray matter
3. break off, come back

IV. Making Sense of Sentences
Sample Answers
1. This article tells readers that dolphins are less lovable than previously thought.
2. The social alliances of dolphins are more sophisticated than scientists realized in the past.
3. The alliances of chimpanzees are less complex than those of dolphins.
4. Scientists say that female dolphins are more difficult to understand than males.

Science and Environment: Article 4

The Latest Riddle of the Sphinx

I. Getting the Message
B.

3000 B.C.: rise of Egyptian civilization

7000-5000 B.C.: period when the Sphinx may have been built according to the latest research

9000 B.C.: date in which a large construction project was completed in Jericho; it shows people of the time were capable builders.

II. Expanding Your Vocabulary

A. Getting Meaning from Context

1. a	4. a	7. b
2. b	5. b	8. a
3. b	6. a	9. a

B. Study Word Parts

2 a person who studies
6 under, below, beneath
1 ancient, the beginning
5 speech, story, legend
4 earth, of the earth
3 out, from, away from

III. Making Sense of Sentences

Sample Answers

1. If Robert Schoch is correct, the Sphinx is much older than people have traditionally thought.
2. If Mark Lehner is correct, the Sphinx was built by the Pharaoh Khafre about 2500 B.C.
3. If archaeologists knew which pharaoh built the Sphinx, they could date when it was built.
4. If the Sphinx had been made of wood or clay, it would have disappeared long ago because of weathering.
5. If I ever take a trip to Egypt, I will visit the pyramids.
   Items 1, 2, 5 are possibilities.

SECTION 7: SPORTS

Sports: Article I

A Chinese Tennis Player's Uneasy Season

I. Getting the Message

B.

Taiwan: where Hu's sponsor is from

Tiananmen Square: location of demonstrations Hu saw on TV

San Diego: where Hu lives

Chengdu: Hu's hometown

Schenectady, NY: where Hu won her first professional title

Newport, RI: where Hu had her best singles performance of the year, getting to the quarterfinals

II. Expanding Your Vocabulary

A. Getting Meaning from Context

1. b	4. b	7. a
2. a	5. b	8. b
3. b	6. b	

B. Defining Useful Vocabulary

6 a few
3 attacking
4 not the best or the worst
2 position in relation to others
5 cut off, stopped
1 get, reach

C. Practicing Useful Vocabulary

1. aggressive, middle-level
2. attain, severed
3. ranking, a handful

D. Reading for Suggested Meanings

1. *Rumblings* refers to the reports of political unrest in China.
2. *Victims* seems an exaggerated word to describe an opponent that one has defeated.
3. *Keep your eye on the ball* is often used figuratively to mean "concentrate." Here what Hu has to concentrate on is an actual tennis ball.
4. a. The TV images of political unrest in China come into her eyes.
   b. This makes it difficult for her to

keep her eye on the ball and concentrate.

III. Making Sense of Sentences

paragraph 4: When I'm playing I'm concentrating on tennis

paragraph 5: For a while after she defected to the United States in 1982, Hu was an embarrassment to the Chinese government.

Answers will vary.

Sports: Article 2

In Europe, It's Still Diamonds in the Rough

I. Getting the Message

B. *Sample Answers*

Baseball is now a medal sport at the Olympics; the sport is promoted in some countries, such as the Netherlands

II. Expanding Your Vocabulary

Getting Meaning from Context

1. b	4. b
2. a	5. a
3. a	6. a

III. Working with Idioms

1. The European baseball championships were going to be held in Paris once the finishing touches were put on the field.
2. Italy opened up to outside influences during and after World War II. Many things from other cultures like baseball were introduced into Italy.
3. At least one European made it to the major leagues.
4. The Olympics is out of reach to most European teams since only three European teams can compete in the Olympics.

IV. Making Sense of Sentences

1. because we know how to sell it and how to educate our audience through the media
2. *Answers will vary.*

Sports Article 3

Man Still Beats Chess Machine, for Now

I. Getting the Message

B.

1. Deep Thought
2. Kasparov
3. Deep Thought
4. Kasparov

II. Expanding Your Vocabulary

Getting Meaning from Context

1. a	5. b	9. b
2. b	6. a	10. a
3. a	7. b	
4. b	8. a	

III. Working with Idioms

1. Computers can now beat grandmasters of chess, so human supremacy may be ending.
2. Computers are becoming better chess players, and Kasparov is not eager to play the more powerful, intelligent computers.
3. No. The computer was run by scientists who developed the computer.
4. The scientists did not think that Deep Thought would win. The best they thought could happen was a tie, or a draw.

5. The computer was not a strong opponent for Kasparov, and so people wondered if there was something wrong with the computer.

IV. Making Sense of Sentences

1. players (first occurrence)
2. computer
3. machine (that can scan a billion positions a second)
4. a human player

Sample Answers

1. The computer scientists hoped that Deep Thought would do well, but they (scientists) expected Kasparov to beat it (Deep Thought).
2. Kasparov challenged Deep Thought because he (Kasparov) wanted to show that the human mind is stronger than a computer.
3. At the end, Kasparov's opinion of Deep Thought was that it (Deep Thought) was not a very strong opponent for him (Kasparov).

Sports: Article 4

Downhill Racers: Taking On the Mountain at Any Risk

I. Getting the Message

B. *Sample Answers*

Positive: It gives a feeling of freedom practicing the sport; it gives personal satisfaction to conquer the hill. Negative: There are not very many monetary rewards; the sport can be very dangerous and even fatal.

II. Expanding Your Vocabulary

Getting Meaning from Context

1. a	4. b	7. b
2. b	5. a	8. b
3. a	6. a	9. b

III. Working with Idioms

1. *At any risk* suggests the person is willing to face any danger.
2. Klammer is remembering, or looking back on, his victory in the downhill in the 1976 Olympics.
3. Johnson knew that his days were numbered and that his career was almost finished, when he lost his concentration and confidence for a tenth of a second.
4. Johnson knew his day would come when he saw the large crowd waiting to see the Olympic race and felt the excitement. He was anticipating becoming a famous skier himself.
5. Irwin was left with a severe concussion and a fractured rib.

IV. Focusing on Style and Tone

Sample Answers

"a slow-motion effect" (paragraph 6)
"a feeling of freedom" (paragraph 7)